HONOLULU
MAGAZINE'S

THE
GREATEST HAWAI'I ALBUMS
50

HONOLULU MAGAZINE'S

THE GREATEST 50 HAWAI'I ALBUMS

Ronna Bolante
and Michael Keany

WATERMARK
PUBLISHING

A portion of the proceeds from the sale of this book supports the Hawaiian Music Hall of Fame.

ISBN 0-9753740-1-X

Library of Congress Control Number: 2004114829
Design by Leo Gonzalez
Design/production by Nancy Watanabe

Watermark Publishing
1088 Bishop Street, Suite 310
Honolulu, HI 96813
Telephone: Toll-free 1-866-900-BOOK
Web site: www.bookshawaii.net
e-mail: sales@bookshawaii.net

Printed in the Republic of Korea

Many thanks to John Heckathorn and Scott Schumaker of HONOLULU Magazine for their support and encouragement, and to Harry B. Soria, Jr., who has been an invaluable resource. Mahalo also to our esteemed panelists for creating such a dynamic list, and to all the artists, family members, producers and others who shared their stories with us. We couldn't have done it without you.

Ronna Bolante
and Michael Keany

CONTENTS

The 50 Greatest Hawai'i Albums

FOREWORD

Hawai'i's music is essentially the story of its people – their genealogy, their love of the land and sea, their aloha for each other and for those who visit these beautiful islands. Our musical connections go back over the generations to the time of our ancestors – the Kamehameha and Kalākaua families, the ranching and plantation pioneers who left their mark on the landscape, and all the hard-working people who built these Islands with their hands and hearts.

In my case, I was blessed with many exceptional teachers, legendary musicans such as Bill Lincoln, Vickie I'i Rodrigues, Alice Namakelua, Lei Collins, Bina Mossman, Kawena Puku'i, Maddy Lam and the great Madame Alapa'i, my *hānai* grandmother, the first female singer of the Royal Hawaiian Band and a favorite artist at the court of King Kalākaua. In true Hawaiian fashion, these aunties and uncles gave freely of themselves because we were all family, and passing their gift of music along was their way of *aloha*. It was all so intimate: we were able to live the music, and to celebrate our history and our own lives through it as well.

Today, as the message and beauty of Hawaiian music has been carried around the world, I feel privileged to have been a part of its renaissance and its continued growth. Over the years I've taught music to many people. Regardless of who you are or where you come from, if you love Hawai'i's music and you are sincere about learning it properly, then I will be there to teach you. It has been my life's work, and I pray to God that I am able to continue until the day I die.

My hope for the young musicians of Hawai'i is that they be given the same love and support that I enjoyed. That's the Hawaiian style, and that's why we founded the Hawaiian Music Hall of Fame. It has been a wonderful way to showcase our Island musicians, and to perpetuate for our youth the beautiful music that came before us.

This same spirit – this connection between past and future – is evident in this book, *The 50 Greatest Hawai'i Albums*. This very special collection goes a long way toward preserving our musical tradition and introducing it, with much aloha, to the next generation.

Kahauanu Lake

Hawaiian Music Hall of Fame

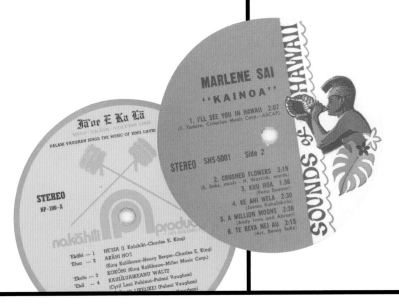

INTRODUCTION

In June 2004, HONOLULU Magazine published an issue devoted to "The 50 Greatest Hawai'i Albums of All Time."

It was one of our most popular – and controversial – issues ever. It spawned much discussion, not to mention a CD, a television special and now a book.

We didn't anticipate any of that. We simply wanted to remind people in Hawai'i of how great Island music is. How often we take it for granted, when we should be celebrating it.

Hawai'i is the only state with its own distinctive music. Inspired by the landscape and the indigenous Hawaiian culture, the music of the Islands draws inspiration from around the world. It incorporates influences from sources as diverse as country-western and reggae, all the while remaining distinctively itself.

How did we take this large body of music and create a list of only 50 albums? By enlisting a panel of 12 distinguished members of the Hawai'i music community (following pages). One note: we had badly wanted to include Krash Kealoha, founder of the Nā Hōkū Hanohano awards, to be one of the judges. However, illness kept Krash from participating. At the last minute, I was forced, reluctantly, to take his place on the panel.

Then, each panelist drew up his or her own list of artistically successful and historically important albums.

Note that the list was of Hawai'i albums, not individual songs. That meant we began with the 33-1/3 LP records of the early 1950s and continued to the CDs of today.

In addition, we asked for the best *Hawai'i* music albums, not the best Hawaiian albums. We recognize that without the Hawaiian language and musical sensitivity, Hawai'i music might have disappeared into the mainstream generations ago. Still, we wanted to avoid arguments about whether any particular album was "truly Hawaiian." To us, it didn't matter, as long as it truly was music of the Islands. We asked the panelists for albums by Hawai'i-based artists, of whatever ethnicity, born here or not, lyrics in Hawaiian or not.

The final list doesn't really reflect any single judge's choices. It's a consensus of many minds. We're proud of the final list; it's a distinguished one. It covers albums from traditional to contemporary, from a whole range of styles.

Once the list was complete, the original magazine article was written by two young, talented HONOLULU staffers, Ronna Bolante and Michael Keany. They had a ball writing it. "I just talked to Don Ho for two hours," they'd say. Or, "I met Palani Vaughan at the Royal Mausoleum." There were more stories than they could tell in the space we gave them, so they have now expanded their work into a book.

We are pleased to capture in print some of the stories behind these albums – before some of those memories disappear. And I am hoping that this book will encourage people to really listen to the music around them. Because it's great music.

John Heckathorn

Editor
HONOLULU
Magazine

MEET THE PANELISTS

The dozen industry experts who rated the records, each with a favorite Hawai'i album that didn't make the cut.

Kapono Beamer

Kapono Beamer

A singer, songwriter and slack-key master, Kapono Beamer has been immersed in Hawaiian music since birth. Perhaps most widely known, along with his brother Keola, as the artist behind *Honolulu City Lights*, Kapono has more than earned his place in the musical dynasty that is the Beamer family.

Kapono's Pick: *Hawai'i's Ed Kenney*, Ed Kenney. "He was my calabash uncle, so I saw his talent firsthand – and he was one of Hawai'i's finest. He even performed on Broadway."

Leah Bernstein

Leah Bernstein

Leah Bernstein is president of local recording and distribution label Mountain Apple Co. In the course of her career, she has worked for recording studios, recording and publishing divisions of major labels and as a traffic girl at KPOI Radio in its heyday. Bernstein has been with the Mountain Apple Co. since 1980, when she began as a receptionist.

Leah's Pick: *Master of Touch and Tone*, Jerry Byrd. "Jerry Byrd is one of the masters of steel guitar, and he brings such a passion to the music that I really felt he should be represented. He's played with everyone from Roy Orbison to Elvis Presley."

Robert Cazimero

Robert Cazimero

A vocalist and bassist, and half of the Brothers Cazimero, Robert is one of Hawaiian music's most respected musicians, with a career that has spanned some 40 years. He appears several times on this list, both with his brother and as part of The Sunday Manoa.

Robert's Pick: "What's missing, in my opinion? Can't think of a one. I'm thrilled to see those listed."

John Heckathorn

It was Heckathorn, as editor of HONOLU-LU Magazine, who came up with the idea for the June 2004 cover story, "The 50 Greatest Hawai'i Albums of All Time." Not a member of the original panel, John stepped in when health problems prevented the legendary radio personality Krash Kealoha from participating.

John's Pick: *Mākaha Bash 3 – Live at the Shell*, Mākaha Sons of Ni'ihau. "Not only is it really talented, but it's incredibly light-hearted. For me, it's the one record where Israel Kamakawiwo'ole's personality really shines through. Plus, what other group could combine 'Uwehe 'Ami And Slide' and 'Curley Shuffle' together in one medley?"

Nina Kealiiwahamana

Nina is one of Hawaii's most elegant singers, a classically trained soprano who was a regular on the historic "Hawai'i Calls" radio show from 1957 until its last broadcast in 1974. She is also well known for her collaboration with composer Jack de Mello.

Nina's Pick: Anything by Haunani Kahalewai. "Alfred Apaka is the male voice of Hawai'i, and Haunani is the epitome of the female voice. She had a three-octave range, and she used it. Whether she sang chalanagalang with the *'ukulele* or 'Paoakalani' as Queen Lili'uokalani intended it, she was magnificent."

Lydia Ludin

Ludin has been a respected Hawaiian music resource for many years. In 2003, her work at the House of Music earned her a Nā Hōkū Hanohano Lifetime Achievement Award.

Lydia's Pick: *Best of Linda*, Linda Dela Cruz. "Lena Machado was known as 'Hawai'i's song bird,' and Linda was 'Hawai'i's canary.' Her voice was almost like Lena's, so powerful. She attended McKinley High School with me and would entertain us at assemblies. She didn't even need a mike."

John Heckathorn

Nina Kealiiwahamana

Lydia Ludin

Tom Moffat

Jacqueline Rossetti

Jake Shimabukuro

Tom Moffatt

Over the past 50 years, Tom Moffatt has become a fixture on the local music and entertainment scene. He began his career as a disc jockey at KPOI Radio when rock 'n roll was in its infancy, and went on to produce and manage local talent such as the Beamer brothers and Country Comfort. He has also been Hawaii's most prolific promoter, booking everyone from the Beach Boys to Michael Jackson.

Tom's Pick: *Cool Heat*, Ethel Azama. "She's probably the best singer that ever came out of Hawai'i. She was more jazz-oriented, and this album came out on Liberty Records, produced by Marty Paich, one of the top arrangers in Hollywood. I have to mention her because whenever I talk to musicians and bring up her name, they just stop, because she's so well-respected."

Jacqueline Rossetti (the Honolulu Skylark)

One of Hawai'i's most recognized radio personalities, Skylark has been a long-time champion of Hawaiian music, hosting a traditional Hawaiian music program on KCCN Radio for more than 20 years. She is a deejay with KHUI 99.5 FM and a board member of the Hawai'i Academy of Recording Arts.

Skylark's Pick: *The Musical Saga of the Hōkūle'a*, Roland Cazimero and the Hōkūle'a Band. "Keli'i Tau'a, Roland Cazimero, Mike Kaawa and Dwight Hanohano were progressive in the recording, and innovative and timely in capturing the spirit of the Hōkūle'a's successful voyage to Tahiti in 1976. The album helped to remind our people of a once proud, strong enduring nation."

Jake Shimabukuro

Shimabukuro first rose to prominence in the late '90s as a member of Pure Heart. After the group's breakup, though, he became a star in his own right as his virtuoso 'ukulele skills propelled him to international fame.

Jake's Pick: *Acoustic Soul*, John Cruz. "As far as recording, there has never been another album that has come out of Hawai'i of this caliber – the way the album was mixed, the arrangement of each song, the songwriting – and the musicians were just monster players. John Cruz himself is really an amazing artist, one of my heroes. He's all about playing from the heart."

Harry B. Soria, Jr.

Harry B. Soria, Jr., the third generation of a local radio dynasty that included his father and grandfather, carries on the tradition as host of "Territorial Airwaves" on 105 KINE radio. He is also a historian with an encyclopedic knowledge of Hawaiian music and its musicians.

Harry's Pick: *On The Rocks*, The Surfers. "They took harmony parts in a new direction from the end of the 1950s and the beginning of the 1960s, sort of taking the torch from The Invitations. A more casual, less lush approach."

Byron Yasui

Yasui teaches composition and music theory as a professor at the University of Hawaii at Mānoa. He practices what he preaches, too – he is well regarded as a classical and jazz bassist.

Byron's Pick: *Songs of Liliuʻokalani*, The Galliard String Quartet, 1995. "It presented music in a classic style. It wasn't a blockbuster, but it's very tasteful music done in a style I don't think has been done before."

Alan Yoshioka

Alan Yoshioka is a music historian with an encyclopedic knowledge of Hawaiian music, as well as vice president of Harry's Music Store and a board member of the Hawaiʻi Academy of Recording Arts.

Alan's Pick: *Rhythm of the Islands*, Karen Keawehawaiʻi. "The album that not only established Karen as a versatile vocalist but more so as a favorite entertainer is the memorable *Rhythm of the Islands*, which took us on a nostalgic musical journey back to the days of the swingin' big bands and the cellophane hula skirt dancers."

Harry B. Soria, Jr.

Byron Yasui

Alan Yoshioka

1

HONOLULU CITY LIGHTS
Keola & Kapono Beamer, 1978

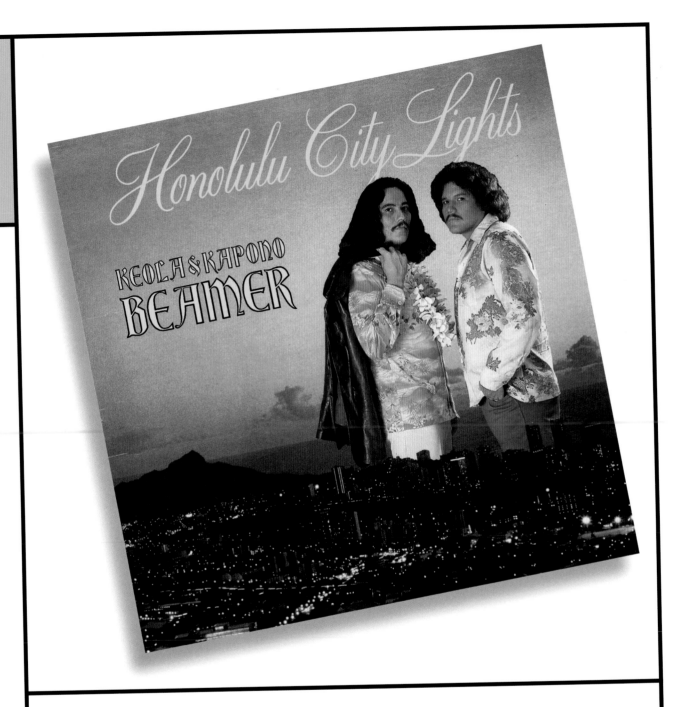

- *Honolulu City Lights*
- *Kaliponi Slack Key*
- *Pauoa Liko Ka Lehua*
- *Love You All the Time*
- *Kamakani Ka 'Ili Aloha*
- *Seabreeze (Puamana)*
- *Nanakuli*
- *Please Let Me Know*
- *Pua Tubarose*
- *Only Good Times (The Three Friends Theme)*

Few albums have become so completely integrated into the consciousness of local culture as Keola and Kapono Beamer's *Honolulu City Lights*. In the 26 years since its release, the songs on it have simply become the soundtrack to Hawai'i.

By now, every man, woman and child in Honolulu has surely given the shaka for the Channel Two news camera at least twice, to the strains of "Kaliponi Slack Key." The album's last track, "Only Good Times," has become a staple of local high school graduations (movie trivia: the song also appears in the surf flick *Big Wednesday*).

And then, of course, there's the title track. Tom Moffatt likes to tell the story about the first time he heard the song "Honolulu City Lights." He was about to sign the Beamer brothers as the first act on his new record label, and Keola called him up one day to say he should come up to 'Alewa Heights to listen to a new song.

"It was late in the afternoon, just as the sun was going down," Moffatt remembered. "The lights were starting to come on, and Keola started to play 'Honolulu City Lights' for me. That was the first time I heard it, just the raw version, and I knew we had a winner right there. I just flipped. It was one of those moments you never forget, hearing that song and looking out over the city — Holy cow."

When the album was released, the rest of Hawai'i said *Holy cow*, as well. "It was just overwhelming when it came out," radio personality Harry B. Soria, Jr., enthused. "It was so full and so lush and so perfect."

Much of that lushness was due to pro-ducer Teddy Randazzo, who wrote and conducted the string arrangements throughout the album. Kapono Beamer said, "Teddy was the best thing that could ever have happened to us. He could see the core of what we were — two guitarists and two vocalists — and he never lost sight of that. Everything he did just embellished the core of the songs."

On the song "Honolulu City Lights," Keola and Kapono's uncle Mahi Beamer added a descending piano counter melody that may sound very familiar to fans of traditional Hawaiian music. It was, in fact, the melody from "To You," written by the renowned Helen Desha Beamer. Randazzo built the string arrangement around that piano part, uniting the new with the old.

Randazzo was also something of a perfectionist, which was all to the good for the Beamers. "He drew out some good performances from us in the studio," Kapono agreed.

Following the success of **Honolulu City Lights,** *Keola (left) and Kapono traveled to Papeete to record* Tahiti Holiday, *also produced by Tom Moffatt.*

"I think that's the hardest we had worked to that point. We'd sing a couple takes, and I thought it sounded OK, but Teddy would make us sing it again. He wasn't mean-spirited about it; he just expected a lot."

Some of the recording was done in Honolulu, but the strings and many of the background parts needed to be done in Los Angeles.

next day or something, but we mixed all those songs in an all-night burnout. But it turned out OK."

The album quickly endeared itself to the hearts of Hawai'i residents and visitors, probably because they recognized the authentic nature of the songwriting. The lyrics of the title track, for example, come not from some imaginary scenario, but from

Another **Honolulu City Lights** *follow-up,* **Island Night***, was recorded using the state-of-the-art facilities of Media Sound Studios in New York City.*

Once everything was on tape, Randazzo and the Beamers mixed the entire album in one marathon 24-hour session at Conway Recording Studio. "We stayed up all night," said Kapono. "I don't know why – Teddy must have had something scheduled the

experience. Keola was inspired to write the song on the eve of an extended trip to California.

"I was getting ready to fly over, and I was looking out over the lights of Honolulu and not really wanting to go that much," he reminisced. "I'm a Hawaiian through and through, and it's difficult to leave the place you love, and so the first seeds of that song were planted in my heart right then, as I looked out over the city from 'Alewa Heights."

The Beamers supported the album by playing a regular gig in the Monarch Room at the Royal Hawaiian Hotel in Waikīkī. After its release, their popularity warranted a new venue, and the Beamers opened up their own show at the Ocean Showroom right on the water at the Reef Hotel.

The next album had a lot to live up to, and the Beamers and Moffat decided to spare no expense in the attempt. Keola said, "I think we went a little nuts. We went to New York and recorded in this really outstanding studio up on Central Park West with a big-name producer. We were trying new stuff and spending all of Tom's money and all kinds of stuff, but it just didn't have that connection that *City Lights* did."

Indeed, *Honolulu City Lights* seemed to be an impossible act to follow, and in 1980 the Beamers broke up to pursue individual careers, ostensibly because of artistic fatigue.

Keola said he was gratified by the enduring response to "Honolulu City Lights." "I was writing about my experience, not the common experience of a human being getting on a plane for parts unknown and watching the jewels of the Islands disappear," he said. "I was just writing the story that was in my heart. Turns out, it lived in many hearts."

Tahiti Holiday, *a salute to the Beamers' Tahitian ancestors, included a remake of the* Honolulu City Lights *classic* "Seabreeze (Puamana)."

2

GUAVA JAM
The Sunday Manoa, 1971

- *Kawika*
- *Only You*
- *Hehe Waipi'o*
- *Kaulana 'O Waimanalo*
- *Ka'ililauokekoa*
- *Mehameha*
- *He Hawai'i Au*
- *Maika'i Ka Makani O Kohala*
- *Ka La'i 'Opua*
- *Poli Pumehana*
- *Guava Jam*

The Sunday Manoa didn't intend to start a revolution. But when the group released *Guava Jam* in 1971, they did. In a decade in which Mainland rock 'n' roll dominated the Islands' radio stations and nightclub scene, *Guava Jam* breathed new life into Hawaiian music. It was the album that launched the Hawaiian Renaissance of the 1970s – a cultural reawakening driven by such music innovators as Gabby Pahinui and the Sons of Hawaii.

"It was really the events of the time that made this album," said Peter Moon, founder of The Sunday Manoa. "We were surprised at how the album was received, because we didn't set out to change anything."

Timing wasn't the only reason *Guava Jam* became a turning point for Hawaiian music. The Sunday Manoa's members were phenomenal. A force on the 'ukulele and slack-key guitar, Moon blazed his way through songs like "Kawika" and the album's title track. Robert and Roland Cazimero's soaring voices and musical dexterity are also imprinted on each song, including the classic "Only You."

"They put our own music back on the pedestal," said radio personality Honolulu Skylark. "Now it was cool to listen to Hawaiian music. They just stole the hearts of our people. I remember the lines to see them at the Sheraton Hotel Prow Lounge. When they performed at the University of Hawai'i, masses of kids packed into Andrew's Amphitheatre, waiting in long lines just to get in."

In a sense, *Guava Jam* became the first truly contemporary Hawaiian album. The Sunday Manoa maintained the integrity of traditional Hawaiian lyrics, but rather than eschewing Western influences, the group embraced them, incorporating them into their own music.

Who else would have thought to give a modern spin to an ancient Hawaiian chant like "Kawika"? The groundbreaking track opens slowly, with traditional *ipu*-like beats that are soon accompanied by Moon's picking on his 'ukulele, then Robert's haunting vocals.

The Sunday Manoa (left to right: Roland Cazimero, Peter Moon and Robert Cazimero) was a popular draw on the Island entertainment scene. The trio played Waikīkī nightclubs, the University of Hawai'i's Andrews Amphitheatre and the Big Island's Waimea Music Festival, among other venues.

"They took the framework of contemporary music and put it inside traditional Hawaiian music like 'Kawika,'" explained longtime radio host Harry B. Soria, Jr. "They shook up the whole thing. Suddenly, Hawaiian music was palatable, and we were able to bridge over to it as young people. Suddenly this was speaking to us, because it was our beat."

Guava Jam wasn't the first album by the group known as The Sunday Manoa. Initially, Moon recruited Palani Vaughan, Cyril Pahinui and Albert "Baby" Kalima to play in the band, even recording two successful albums with them. The name came from a misprint in a Hawaiian songbook, which incorrectly labeled the song "Sunny Manoa" as "Sunday Manoa."

While the players changed, Moon always remained the nucleus of the band. His collaboration with the Cazimero brothers, however, is the lineup Hawai'i music listeners tend to associate with The Sunday Manoa.

"In those days, Peter was a hungry guy," said Hula Records' Don McDiarmid, Jr., who produced *Guava Jam*. "He was very aggressive, and he wanted to make sure everybody knew he was leading the pile. Peter did whatever he felt like doing, whatever came off the top of the hat."

The virtuosity of *Guava Jam* was even more impressive considering the rudimentary recording technology available at the time. Equipment was analog. Overdubbing was unheard of. There were no computers to cut a good note from one session to replace an off note on another. When McDiarmid wanted to fix a section on a

Robert, Roland and Peter (right center) pose with friends in this memorable photo from the Guava Jam *album jacket.*

song, he manually spliced the recording.

"If people listen to 'Kawika,' they can hear Peter just flying on the *'ukulele*," McDiarmid said. "When Peter played, I just kept telling him, 'Keep going. Don't stop,' and he didn't know where the hell he was gonna go. He played wherever his fingers were going. We started editing from the first cut we did."

Guava Jam's recording sessions were a lesson in improvisation. Like Moon, Robert and Roland sometimes deviated from the songs' original arrangements. If they came up with new ideas in the middle of recording, they followed their instincts.

"I could tell this album was completely different from any other album done before, from the first song we did," McDiarmid said. "At that stage, everybody was kind of loose, and they were taking chances. They tried stuff they'd never tried before. On 'Kawika,' Robert started banging the back of his bass, like an *ipu* sound – that worked. It was all extemporaneous."

Public response was immediate and immense. During the renaissance of the 1970s, Hawaiian music suddenly became *the* mainstream music in Hawai'i. Young listeners stopped looking to the Mainland for the next big thing. The excitement was right here at home. And Sunday Manoa stood at its forefront.

"It just happened so quickly, and it was so exciting to watch, because people who had been on the fringe but had never considered getting into it, now they had an avenue, they could go into this middle-of-the-road contemporary Hawaiian music and

rediscover the routes of their families' songs," Soria recalled. "It was just amazing the way it all played it out. It was like a big flower opening up."

More than 30 years after *Guava Jam's* release, the Cazimeros are still floored by the album's longstanding impact.

"When I think about it today, it was just one of the strangest things that ever happened to us, but we're just so happy it did," Robert said. "People still ask me what it was like being at the forefront of the Hawaiian Renaissance, but we didn't realize it. We were just having a good time playing music."

Hula Records' Don McDiarmid, Jr., with wife Alva: "When Peter played, I just kept telling him, 'Keep going. Don't stop,' and he didn't know where the hell he was gonna go. He played wherever his fingers were going."

3

GABBY
Gabby Pahinui, 1972

- *Hiʻilawe (1947) /Luau Hula*
- *Lihue*
- *Heʻeia*
- *Ka Makani Ka ʻIli Aloha*
- *Lei Ohu*
- *Royal Hawaiian Hotel*
- *Keawaiki*
- *Leahi*
- *Wai O Ke Aniani*
- *Kaʻahumanu*
- *Lei Nani*
- *Lei No Kaʻiulani*
- *Ka Moaʻe*
- *Hula O Makee*
- *Hame Pila*
- *Hiʻilawe (1972) /Aloha ʻOe*

Since the creation of this LP, no Hawaiian artist has made more of an impact than Gabby Pahinui. His gravelly, salt-of-the-earth baritone seemed born out of ancient Hawai'i, but his instrumentation was fresh and progressive, bringing new life to the historic songs he played.

Pahinui was a master of the steel guitar – and pretty much any other instrument he fancied picking up. But he became famous for pioneering the modern era of *kī hō'alu* (slack key guitar). Many of the Islands' music greats, including Peter Moon and Kapono Beamer, consider Pahinui one of their biggest influences.

"Gabby was at the forefront of everything that was pointing to the renaissance of Hawaiian music in the 1970s," Beamer said. "I realized I didn't need mainstream pop music like Santana, because we had Gabby right here at home in Hawai'i. He set off a light in my creative spirit. He made me want to play Hawaiian music."

Pahinui became a legend while he was still alive. There's no shortage of incredible tales about this iconic figure, a self-taught musician who never took a single lesson. Some stories tell of Pahinui's uncanny ear for music. There was the time he played a three-month stint with a 12-piece dance band in Waikīkī before the group realized Pahinui could not read a single note of music.

There's another story about how Pahinui sat in on a rehearsal of several studio musicians tapped to play on one of his albums. The musicians all belonged to the prestigious Los Angeles Philharmonic. But

Pahinui, who had no such classical training, insisted that one of them was out of tune. Remarkably, he was right. When the seasoned musicians finished rehearsing, they lined up to shake Pahinui's hand.

"He could play upside-down, backward, any way – he was spectacular," enthused Don McDiarmid, Jr., who produced Pahinui's first album with the band Sons of Hawaii on Hula Records. "That's why he has that legend that just follows him around like a cloud. He'd show up anyplace and do all kinds of things."

In addition to his extraordinary musical talent, Pahinui knew how to have a good time. His Bell Street home in Waimānalo was known for its weekly backyard parties. The festivities lasted from Friday afternoon

At Keawa'iki on the Big Island, the three members of Panini Productions (left to right: Lawrence Brown, Steve Siegfried and Witt Shingle) talk story with Gabby during a recording session for the Gabby Pahinui Hawaiian Band albums, produced by Panini after the release of Gabby.

to Sunday night, with music playing and alcohol flowing the entire time. Guests often included some of Hawai'i's top musicians, including Andy Cummings and Eddie Kamae.

"He could stay up for three days, drinking and playing music for Hawaiians and non-Hawaiians alike," said Pahinui's son, Bla. "As long as people were listening, he'd stay up all night."

Of course, Pahinui's drinking habits weren't usually good for business. He was known to miss gigs if he was having too much fun somewhere else. Or he might get a little too tipsy during a performance. But even then, drinking never impaired his ability to play.

"Gabby was working for the city and county road crew for a number of years, and we would pick him up right after work for

the rehearsals," said Steve Siegfried, who co-produced *Gabby* with Witt Shingle and Lawrence Brown. "We [used to go] down to the county yard, wait for him to punch out and pick him up. If he had to wait, he'd start drinking."

While Pahinui was a free spirit, he was serious about his music.

"He was pretty strict," Siegfried said. "If you played the wrong note, believe me, he told you. He'd say, 'Oh, you hit a blue one,' and everyone would cringe, waiting to see who it was."

Gabby marked the start of Pahinui's music-making with his sons Martin, Bla, Cyril and Philip. Each son's musical style and tastes left their impact on this album. Martin, for instance, was heavily influenced by the Beatles. Bla, who plays left-handed, with the guitar upside down, gravitated toward the doo-wop groups of the '50s.

"Most musicians would be intimidated by playing with younger kids, especially their own, but Gabby was always open to stuff," Siegfried said. "That was one of the great things about him. If you played something he liked, he embraced it."

Gabby, often called *The Brown Album*, featured an unprecedented lineup of six stellar guitarists – Pahinui, his four sons and Leland "Atta" Isaacs – as well as bassist Manuel "Joe Gang" Kupahu. New recording technology enabled Panini to record the album using eight tracks, much more versatile than the two to four tracks Pahinui was used to. That flexibility gave Pahinui room to experiment, allowing him to play more than one instrument or sing more than one part on a single song.

Although Pahinui had already become a local cult figure while working with the Sons of Hawaii, this album charted a new path. *Gabby* introduced him to a larger, international audience. It also brought more

The stellar lineup of guitarists on Gabby included Manuel "Joe Gang" Kupahu and Gabby's son Martin (left to right, at left) and Leland "Atta" Isaacs (bottom).

authentic Hawaiian music to the rest of the world.

The Brown Album features two versions of Pahinui's signature piece, "Hi'ilawe." One version is among his earliest recordings, done in 1947 when he was 26 years old. The second rendition, the album's final track, was recorded in 1972, on his 51st birthday.

"There were a lot of great entertainers who came and went, but Gabby was so different," Bla remembered. "If you were sitting next to him, you would feel it, the way this guy thinks, how he presents himself, what he says. You wanted to follow this guy. When he went on stage, people would cry. That's gone, you don't see that anymore."

Martin says tourists still venture out to Waimānalo to take pictures of Pahinui's Bell Street home, more than 20 years after he died. Through his music, Gabby Pahinui has achieved immortality. "I didn't realize how big my father was until he died," Martin marvelled. "He's not just big here, but all over the world."

THE EXTRAORDINARY KUI LEE

Kui Lee, 1966

4

- *I'll Remember You*
- *Rain, Rain Go Away*
- *Yes, It's You*
- *Kamakani Ka 'Ili Aloha*

- *Goin' Home*
- *Ain't No Big Thing*
- *Na 'Ali'i*
- *The Days Of My Youth*
- *All I Want To Do*

- *If I Had to Do It All Over Again*
- *Get On Home*
- *No Other Song*

Kui Lee is known as the songwriter who helped catapult Don Ho to fame, by penning such hits as "I'll Remember You" and "One Paddle Two Paddle." His debut album, *The Extraordinary Kui Lee*, didn't just reinforce his reputation as a songwriter. It also proved that Lee was a sharp song stylist, capable of rockin' with the best of 'em.

The Extraordinary Kui Lee was released in November 1966, just two weeks before the artist died of cancer. This album mixed rock, jazz and R&B to create distinctly cosmopolitan songs, such as "Ain't No Big Thing" and "Rain, Rain Go Away." Considering the timing of the album's release, songs like "The Days of My Youth" and "If I Had to Do It All Over Again" seemed elegiac.

Lee came from a family of entertainers. His father, William "Billy" Lee, sang falsetto. His mother, Ethel Baker Lee, was a dancer, singer and musician. Although Lee was born in Shanghai, he grew up in Hawai'i, attending Kamehameha School and Roosevelt High School.

Lee was usually more interested in surfing than his studies, but he didn't need to hit the books as often as most students. He was naturally intelligent, said Buddy Fo, who served with Lee in the U.S. Coast Guard.

"There were about 50 local boys who joined, and we were all on this ship together," said Fo, a founding member of The Invitations. "He used to read a lot, and he'd to read us all the time, like little children."

Some people considered Lee abrasive or temperamental. "Kui was very intelligent, so people bored him quickly," Fo explained. "At the bar, he would talk to guys and twist their brains around; the guy had a vocabulary that would not quit. He was very talented, very smart, but he upset people quick."

Lee performed on the Mainland for 10 years before working with Don Ho. Lee's genius as a songwriter eclipsed his other accomplishments, including his career as a professional knife dancer and choreographer in such venues as the Lexington Hotel's Hawaiian Room. During those 10 years, Lee frequently returned home to Hawai'i, usually stopping by to visit Ho, another Kamehameha alum, at his family's bar in Kāne'ohe.

"We spent thousands and thousands of hours on the bar, talking about what we thought about the music that was going on in Hawai'i," Ho recalled. "Kui would say to me, 'Don, listen to this song. What you think?'"

Lee respected Ho's musical instincts. While the lyrics to Lee's earliest composi-

Kui Lee: a brilliant songwriter and an Island music legend.

tions were beautiful, Ho said, the melodies weren't up to par.

"He wrote the lyrics, and some other guy wrote all the music," Ho explained. "I said,

Before he was a recording artist, Kui Lee toured the country as an original member of the Samoan Warriors fire knife dance troupe (above, in 1953). Kui later appeared with his flashing knives on The Ed Sullivan Show.

'Kui, why don't you make your own music?' He played within his knowledge. He knew five or six chords, and if he kept the music in his realm, because of its simplicity, it really came out beautiful. That, to me, was the beginning of Kui's beautiful music."

These exchanges also marked the start of a creative partnership between the two friends. Lee expressed to Ho his frustration at how much of Hawai'i's music in those days was written on the Mainland, usually not by Hawaiians. Lee believed that Hawai'i music should come from the Islands and its people and capture the local lifestyle.

Lee returned home for good in the early '60s. "A lot of the concept of the music came from our philosophy of our life, the way we lived on the beach, we were like free spirits," Ho said.

"We would always have a beer every day or always have a party, music with the boys, everybody singing. 'Ain't No Big Thing,' 'Suck 'Em Up' – that was our lifestyle, so he wrote about it."

In the decade before Lee died, he composed about 40 songs. Many of those tunes became Ho's biggest hits; most notably, Lee's signature song, "I'll Remember You."

"The day Kui taught me 'I'll Remember You' is the same day he told me he had throat cancer," Ho recalled. "That night, we met at a friend's apartment, and Kui said to me, 'I got the perfect song for you.' I sat there for four hours and made sure he sang it for me over and over again, so I would get everything right, exactly what he was feeling."

When Ho left the apartment the following morning, he headed straight for Duke's in Waikīkī, where he performed, without any sleep. He wanted to arrange the song on his keyboard and have his band, the Aliis, rehearse the new number.

"I performed the song for the first time that night at Duke's," Ho said. "I told the audience, 'I'd like to sing a beautiful song written by a friend of mine, who has cancer.' I had a hard time getting through the song. I got so choked up, people in the audience started to cry."

Ho called Lee to the stage to perform the song. When Lee finished, there wasn't a dry eye in the house.

That song was released on *The Don Ho Show!* and *Don Ho Again!*, two albums recorded live at Duke's by Reprise Records.

Lee recorded his first album, *The Extraordinary Kui Lee*, just months before his death in 1966. When he started recording sessions at Columbia Records in New York, everyone there knew he'd been told he had six months to live. The album featured some of the best musicians of the '60s, including drummer Bill Lavorgna, guitarist Stuart Scharf and keyboardist Bernie Krause.

"I got to see one of the last performances of Kui Lee before his passing, and it was at the Waikīkī Shell," said longtime radio deejay Honolulu Skylark. "I was 14, and I didn't understand at the time what this frail man was all about. When his album finally came out, I realized the depth of his songwriting abilities. He was very progressive, way before his time. I don't think people realized his talent till he was gone."

While he didn't achieve Don Ho's level of success as an entertainer, Lee proved with this album that he was both a capable song stylist and a brilliant songwriter. All 12 of the album's songs are his original compositions. He died at age 34, but the genius of his songs lives on. "I'll Remember You," for instance, has been recorded dozens of times, most notably by Tony Bennett, Andy Williams and Elvis Presley. Of course, most music buffs agree Ho's version can't be beat.

"Even today, the way I sing that song is exactly the way Kui taught it to me that one night many years ago," Ho said. "Kui was a poet, and I was just the messenger boy."

According to his nephew, professional surfer Reno Abellira, this photo of Kui (right) surfing at Ala Moana was his original choice for the front cover of The Extraordinary Kui Lee*.*

5

KAWAIPUNAHELE
Keali'i Reichel, 1994

- *Kawaipunahele*
- *Oli/In My Life*
- *Hanohano Ka Lei Pikake*
- *If We Hold On Together*
- *E Ho'i I Ka Pili*
- *Wanting Memories*
- *Kauanoeanuhea*
- *Ku'u Wehi O Ke Aumoe*
- *'Akaka Falls*
- *Pua Mikinolia*
- *Come Sail Away*
- *He Mele Inoa No Ka wai punahele-o-Pali-Kū*

With this 1994 debut release, Keali'i Reichel seemed to appear out of nowhere as a fully formed music star. However, the making of *Kawaipunahele* was actually a seat-of-the-pants affair. At the time, Reichel was the executive director of the Bailey House Museum in Wailuku, and was most well known within the hula community, as a respected *kumu hula* of his own *hālau*, Ka Makani Wili Makaha O Kaua'ula.

The extent of his commercial exposure at that point was a choreographing and dancing gig he had had in a *lū'au* show at the Stouffer Wailea Beach Hotel. His friend Jamie Lawrence, who headlined the show, said Reichel shunned the spotlight: "He would set up a chair on the side, and I would tell him, 'Keali'i, come sing with me!' And he would be, 'No, no.' He would take his guitar and sit on a barstool to the side, totally unobtrusive and just kind of playing along with me. Not even plugged in or anything."

At the same time, though, Reichel was quietly writing original songs. "I was going through some really rough times," he said, "and I was composing songs and chants quite a lot. For no particular reason, other than just to do it. So I started singing the songs to myself, in the shower, around the house."

When Reichel's friends began overhearing snatches of "Kawaipunahele" and other songs, they understandably pressured him to record the tunes. Reichel demurred – these were personal expressions, more like diary entries than public material.

The pressure continued. Reichel laughed, "Finally a friend of mine, Fred Krauss, bugged me so much that I said, 'OK, you know what, you guys get the money together, and I'll do it.' And they called my bluff."

His *hālau* sold shortbread cookies and taro bread to raise funds, and Fred's mother, Doris Krauss, also contributed money, enough to finance a modest recording project.

With the money secured, the next step was to find someone with studio know-how. Serendipitously, Reichel's friend Louis "Moon" Kauakahi of the Makaha Sons was at the time recording "Ho'oluana" (number 41 on our list) with renowned producer and engineer Jim Linkner, who had worked with everyone from Olomana to Moe Keale to Brian Wilson.

Linker recalled Kauakahi petitioning him to produce Reichel's album. "Moony kept saying, 'You've got to check out this

Keali'i Reichel: "I said, 'OK, we'll try this for a year.' And we've been doing it ever since."

guy from Maui, Keali'i Reichel.' I was pretty jaded at the time, doing four or five albums at once, didn't want to think of anything new or about developing a new artist."

Keali'i poses during an album photo shoot in a traditional rain cape fashioned from ti leaves.

But after six months of persuasion, Linkner agreed to a meeting with Reichel and Krauss. "They gave me a karaoke cassette [of Reichel singing], with all the reverb on it and everything. So I said, 'I don't know, maybe sometime, but right now I'm in the middle of a bunch of stuff. I'll listen to it and call you back.'"

Even with the karaoke reverb, Linkner was impressed by Reichel's voice, but he said what really won him over was the prospect of getting in at the beginning of an artist's career.

"I thought back on how much fun it was with Olomana, with that first record, and I thought, you know, this might be fun to do," he remembered. "These guys were at the same stage as Olomana was then. So I called him and told him I'd do it."

Half of *Kawaipunahele* was recorded at Linkner's Dolphin Sound studio on O'ahu, but for cost reasons, the rest came together on Maui, at Jamie Lawrence's home studio. "Jim came over and stayed with me at the house and ran the studio," said Lawrence. "We had a ball. Some songs we recorded in the bathroom, others in all parts of the house. Whatever the song required." All in all, Reichel managed to produce the entire album for under $10,000.

As they were recording, Linkner encouraged Reichel and Krauss to start their own record label, to better capitalize on what he believed would be Reichel's imminent success.

Punahele Productions was born, and the label got off to a quick start. They contracted with Mountain Apple Company to distribute the album, and although Jon de Mello originally wanted an initial shipment of 1,200, Linkner said he pushed for 6,600. "Jon asked, 'Why 6,600?' I said, 'Because that's our break-even point.' Jon said, 'OK, 2,200.' So I went ahead and shipped him 6,600."

It turned out to be a wise move: within a

month of its release, *Kawaipunahele* was number one on the sales charts, and it remained there for more than a year. The album remains a steady seller, and is on track to be certified gold.

Reichel's sudden success began encroaching on his formerly private life. People were coming up to see him at his job at the Bailey House Museum, and there was a widespread call for him to perform in support of the album.

presses. And actually my first inclination was to stop the presses, because I really didn't want to do this. It was kind of frightening."

Reichel's friends managed to persuade him that a career in music would allow him to express himself culturally and educate the public about poetry and oral traditions, all while keeping him out of the red.

"I was already doing cultural education and all those kinds of things," he said. "The only thing left was the financial aspect,

For the album cover of Kawaipunahele, Keali'i and the photo crew traveled by helicopter to a spot near Pu'u Kukui, highest peak in the West Maui Mountains.

"I didn't foresee this coming," Reichel said, "and it came to the point where I had to make a decision: to pursue this as a career, which meant performing, or else stop the

which kind of tipped the balance. I said, 'OK, we'll try this for a year.' And we've been doing it ever since."

6

EXOTICA
Martin Denny, 1959

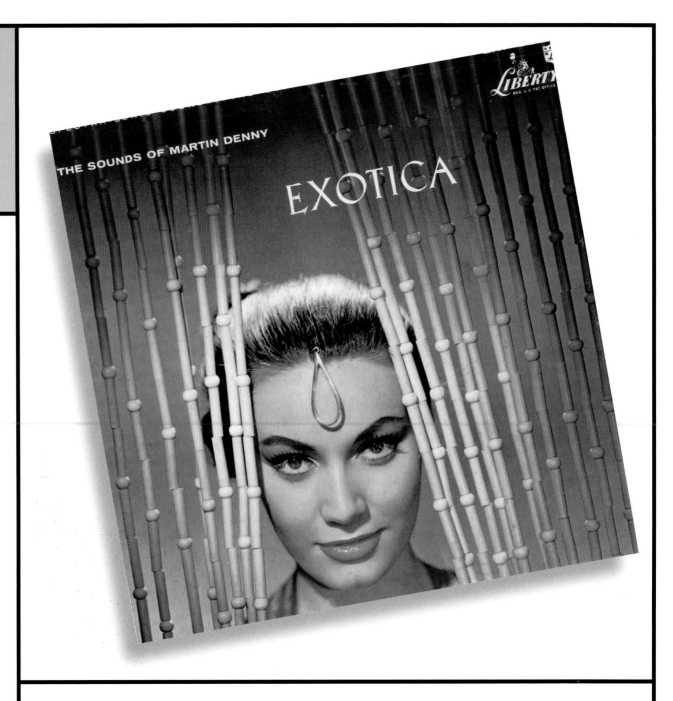

- *Quiet Village*
- *Return To Paradise*
- *Hong Kong Blues*
- *Busy Port*
- *Lotus Land*
- *Similau*
- *Stone God*
- *Jungle Flower*
- *China Nights*
- *Ah Me Furi*
- *Waipio*
- *Love Dance*

To many, Martin Denny *is* exotica. He became an ambassador of the lounge-y, tropical sound in the late 1950s and early '60s, riding the national wave of fascination with the newly admitted state of Hawai'i and taking advantage of the latest in stereo technology.

"Denny's music was instrumental, cocktail music, and yet it was so fascinating that people would sit down and just listen to it," said Harry B. Soria, Jr. "It was high-quality stereo, the latest technology, beautiful bird calls all over your living room. You thought you were in the jungle when Martin's music was playing."

Denny developed the rainforest-evoking style almost by accident, while playing at Henry J. Kaiser's Hawaiian Village Shell Bar in Waikīkī. He noticed one night on stage that frogs in a nearby pond were croaking loudly and in a fit of whimsy began playing around their intermittent calls. The audience loved it, and soon bandmate Augie Colon began throwing enthusiastic birdcalls into the mix. Exotica was born.

An initial mono recording of the album *Exotica* released in 1957 was mildly successful, but two years later, Denny re-recorded the album in stereo with Liberty Records and it became a nationwide hit.

His interpretation of Les Baxter's "Quiet Village," in particular, was a tremendous success, reaching number four on the *Billboard* Top 40 pop chart.

The macaw screeches and bongos might not have been geographically accurate, but they somehow fit the times perfectly. Singer Nina Kealiiwamahana vividly remembered Denny's gigs at the Shell Bar: "He was in a world of his own. It was so perfect for that venue. After you heard Martin Denny, you expected to hear his music each and every time you went into the Tropics or Beachcomber's."

Duke Kahanamoku's in the International Marketplace was one of several Island venues to showcase Martin Denny's exotic sound. Left to right: Martin, Harvey Ragsdale, Julius Wechter, Frank Kim and Augie Colon.

7

YOUNG HAWAII PLAYS OLD HAWAII
Hui Ohana, 1973

- *Nani Waimea*
- *Salomila*
- *E Liliu E*
- *E Mama E*
- *'Ulupalakua*

- *Sweet Lei Mokihana*
- *Ui Lani*
- *Kaloaloa*
- *Pua Lililehua*
- *Nanakuli*

- *Pua Maeole*
- *Hula O Makee Pua*
- *Lilia*

As their name suggests, Hui Ohana were literally a family group – twin brothers Ledward and Nedward Kaapana and their second cousin Dennis Pavao, all from Kalapana on the Big Island. They were hugely prolific during their short career, but this debut album stands out as an embodiment of the Hawaiian Renaissance of the early '70s.

Young Hawaii Plays Old Hawaii is a canny update of old standards, with Led slipping in Ventures surf licks with the traditional slack key, and Pavao's unbelievable falsetto soaring over everything. The "Young Hawaii" part was appropriate in another way; when the album came out in 1973, the Kaapanas were 23 years old, and Dennis Pavao, 21.

The Kaapana brothers grew up surrounded by music. According to Ledward, just about everyone in his family played an instrument or sang. By the age of 16, they were already performing in Hilo nightclubs (accompanied by their parents, of course, because they were underage).

"Growing up, learning the music the way we did, it was so natural. Every time we got together and played, everybody just knew where to go. And if anybody had a hard time, we would just switch places, make it easier," Ledward said.

When they were old enough to move out of the house, Led and Ned moved to Maui to play at Kui Lee's nightclub, the El Dorado. They then spent some time in Los Angeles before returning to Hawai'i to try their luck on O'ahu. "Honolulu – that's where everything was happening," Ledward said. "You came here to record. When I was growing up, I used to listen to Gabby and all them, and think, *Oh man, we should go down there and do the same thing.*"

Fifteen years after the release of Young Hawaii Plays Old Hawaii, *the trio traveled to French Polynesia to make* Tahiti – Come On Over, *produced by Tom Moffatt and recorded at a concert in the Aorai Tinihau Amphitheatre on the outskirts of Papeete. The live album included an updated version of* Young Hawaii's *"Hula O Makee."*

They had been playing with Leonard Pavao, but when he left the group, Led and Ned picked up Leonard's younger brother, Dennis, who was at the time playing drums.

Dennis was a perfect fit for the band: he played a capable rhythm guitar to complement Led's lead guitar and Ned's bass, and he had an amazingly limber falsetto. "We were just like a puzzle," Ledward remembered. "It's hard to find the other piece, but then it just fits right. We wasn't thinking about working hard, we were just enjoying it. The music was just flowing."

Ledward Kaapana: *"Growing up, learning the music the way we did, it was so natural. Every time we got together and played, everybody just knew where to go."*

The trio's started small: their first gig as Hui Ohana in 1968 was at a bowling alley, Leeward Lounge in Pearl City. They soon gained a reputation around town and began appearing regularly on Danny Kaleikini's popular show at the Kahala Hilton. During

the day they worked construction to make ends meet.

In 1973, the group signed a record contract with Bill Murata on Lehua Records. When they got into the studio, they took the same brisk attitude towards recording that they did when playing live: they banged out *Young Hawaii Plays Old Hawaii* in a single day.

"At that time, if you made a mistake, you had to start all over again. Not like today, you make a mistake and you can just patch it. So we hardly made any mistakes," Ledward laughed.

Apparently this wasn't the norm. "The engineer said, 'Hey, you guys better slow down, I'm losing money,'" Ledward said. "We never knew about this kind of stuff. Bill Murata came and told us, 'No, no, you guys are doing fine; you're saving me money.'"

The music was recorded in a hurry, but you'd never be able to tell by listening to it – songs like "'Ulupalakua" and "Nanakuli" have a smooth, rich feel that evokes a summer Sunday afternoon on the back *lanai*.

Hui Ohana kept up their breakneck pace, quickly establishing themselves as the best falsetto group in Hawai'i while popping out more than an album a year until their breakup in 1978 – eight records in all.

As Ledward told it, money complicated the inter-band relationships, distracting them from their first love.

"I would rather we play the music and find the right people to handle the business side, but my brother Ned, he wanted to run the business. He didn't know nothing about business," he explained. "So we used to get

Artist Martin Charlot provided the artwork for the eponymous reunion album Hui Ohana, *released by Tom Moffatt's Paradise Productions in 1987.*

too much problems between the three of us. I told him, no worry about the business, all you gotta do is continue to play music."

Tom Moffat persuaded Hui Ohana to reunite in 1987 to record another album. Their version of "Pua Carnation" won a Hōkū for "Single of the Year" in 1988, but they weren't able to capture the easy grace of their earlier career, and Hui Ohana broke up for good. Each of the members went on to have successful solo careers, although, sadly, Dennis Pavao died in 2002 of a stroke.

Hui Ohana's influence lives on – Led tells the story of a concert at the University of Hawai'i at Mānoa, where he opened up for Bob Dylan. "His backup musicians, all his guitar players, they came up to me and told me, 'Are you the guy that was in that group, Hui Ohana?' I said yeah. They said, 'We listen to that (first) album every chance we get. Wish we could see this group in action.'"

Even decades later, the album still feels both fresh and timeless, a blend of the best of young and old Hawai'i.

8

HOʻĀLA

The Brothers Cazimero, 1978

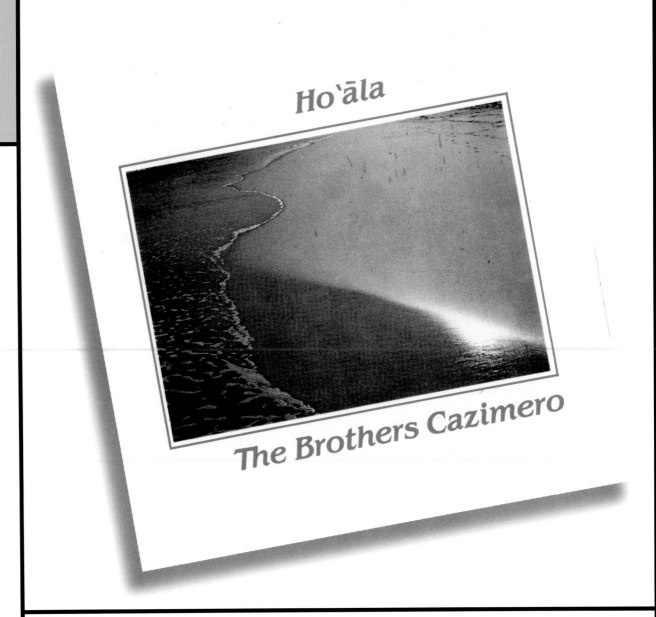

Ho'āla

The Brothers Cazimero

- *Nani Hanalei*
- *Keala*
- *The Beauty of Maunakea*
- *Mu'olaulani*

- *Iʻa Stew (Fish Stew)*
- *Pua Hone*
- *Ka Makani Kaʻili Aloha*
- *Ka ʻUla Laʻau O Kai*

- *Pua Mae'ole*
- *Na Menehune Ekolu*
- *The Breeze and I / Pierre's Song*

Although Robert and Roland Cazimero have recorded more than 30 albums together, *Hoʻāla* remains one of their standouts. Mesmerizing vocals and full-bodied instrumentation – a product of Robert's skill on bass and Roland's mastery of the 12-string guitar – make each song a simple masterpiece.

"We work hard for every album, but *Hoʻāla* was something where working was just not a problem," Robert remembered. "It was like we were guided. We were just instruments."

The place where the brothers recorded *Hoʻāla* had a lot to do with it. Rather than using a typical studio in Honolulu, producer Jon de Mello decided to remove the brothers from the urban grind, setting up a makeshift studio in Hāʻena on Kauaʻi.

Jon rented a beachfront mansion owned by tennis star Billie Jean King. He shipped basic studio equipment, all analog, and instruments to Kauaʻi, holding recording sessions in the mansion's high-ceilinged living room. He also flew in guest artists to join them. From Aug. 27 to Sept. 3 in 1978, Robert, Roland and Jon simply lived the music of *Hoʻāla*.

"It allowed these artists to divorce [themselves from] their daily chores and focus on the songs," Jon recalled. "If we had an idea in the middle of the night, we'd say, 'OK, everybody get up, we're gonna try this.' If there was a bit of stagnant time, I'd call a helicopter, have them drop Roland and Robert off in the middle of the Nā Pali Coast valley with a cooler of food and drinks. They'd go swimming in a waterfall, walk in the valley and come back to the house inspired."

Most of the songs were recorded in the order they appear on the album, giving fluidity to the entire work. The first track,

"Nani Hanalei," for instance, opens with a chant, welcoming listeners in traditional Hawaiian fashion. The final track, "Pierre's Song," wistfully concludes the album with a lilting piano instrumental.

The experience encouraged the brothers to think freely, to act on their musical impulses. The booming *pahu* drum that can be heard on "Nani Hanalei" was actually just a foot-and-a-half tall and a foot wide. Roland came up with the idea of attaching three microphones – two on top, one underneath – to create a more thunderous sound.

Jon headed down to the shore before

Regular fixtures on the Honolulu show scene in the 1970s and '80s, the Brothers Cazimero recorded Hoʻāla *in near-seclusion at Billie Jean King's beachfront home in Hāʻena, Kauaʻi.*

sunrise to record the sounds of the early morning, the waves lapping and the first birds chirping.

A few songs that appear on *Hoʻāla* were written on Kauaʻi, including "Pierre's Song." Robert wrote the tune after taking one of his first trips on a helicopter.

"He called the helicopter the 'chariot of the gods,'" Jon said. "We were weaving in and out of the mountains, through the valleys – Pierre was our pilot. Robert played that song at the house the day after he went flying. When it comes down to it, music is basically a moment in time. They're short performances of life."

Robert and Roland's place in Hawaiian music history began with The Sunday Manoa. Led by Peter Moon, the group produced one of the first albums of the Hawaiian Renaissance, a cultural reawakening that took hold in the early 1970s. The group disbanded in 1973.

After that, "I was in Depressedville," Roland admitted. "No job, no money, not playing anywhere. I was depressed. It's the end. And for a long time, I stayed there."

Then Charlie Thompson, who owned downtown Honolulu hot spot Territorial Tavern, connected the brothers with producer Jack de Mello, Jon's father, who wanted to produce them. Robert and Roland initially wanted to add one more member to the group, but Jack and Jon insisted they'd be stronger as a duo. They were right.

"If you listen to The Sunday Manoa closely, Peter's playing a lot of the leads and frills, the melody work, but the real band and the orchestra is Roland on his 12-string guitar," Jon said. "Roland is probably one of the greatest guitar players in the world, but he's not [just] a guitar player. He's an orchestra. He plays melody, rhythm – he plays all of the orchestral parts."

Jack produced two albums with the Brothers Cazimero before handing the reins to Jon, who had just established his own label, Mountain Apple Co. *Hoʻāla* marked their first collaboration – a creative partnership in its truest sense.

"For me, personally, *Hoʻāla* was my spiritual awakening," Robert said. "It was really when I began to embrace the thought

that I was on this journey and that I had certain expectations made of me and what I made of myself."

The Brothers Cazimero became one of the most enduring, prolific groups in Hawaiian music, and *Hoʻāla* remains one of their favorite albums.

"Whenever we hear the album, we're all right back in the house," Robert said. "I see the piano over there, here's my mic, here's Roland's mic, there's Jon. OK, go. It's quite a memory for us to celebrate, to carry on. Every emotion you can think of happened in that week on Kauaʻi. The magic is on that album."

9

FACING FUTURE

Israel Kamakawiwoʻole, 1993

- Hawaiʻi '78 Introduction
- Ka Huila Wai
- ʻAmaʻama
- Panini Pua Kea
- Take Me Home Country Road
- Kuhio Bay
- Ka Pua Uʻi
- White Sandy Beach of Hawaiʻi
- Henehene Kou ʻAka
- La ʻElima
- Pili Me Kaʻu Manu
- Maui Hawaiian Supʻpa Man
- Kaulana Kawaihae
- Somewhere over the Rainbow / What a Wonderful World
- Hawaiʻi '78

srael Kamakawiwoʻole was the unlikeliest of superstars. Not because of his obesity, although it certainly broke the norm for entertainers in this image-conscience age. But for most of his career, Israel was a member of an ensemble, just one of the Mākaha Sons of Niʻihau. In fact, it was Israel's older brother Skippy who seemed most likely to make it big, until he died in 1982.

Facing Future changed everything, and put Israel squarely into a spotlight that only intensified after his untimely death in 1997. The album was him stretching his wings, on his own for the first time. The public clearly appreciated this transformation, and many also took songs like "Maui Hawaiian Sup'pa Man" and "Hawaiʻi '78" as anthems of a larger political struggle. Whatever con-

text it was viewed in, it was an undisputed triumph, the first Hawaiʻi album to be certified gold.

The artistic and financial success of *Facing Future* certainly validated Israel's decision to leave the Mākaha Sons right after their blockbuster *Hoʻoluana*.

Manager and producer Jon de Mello said Israel originally approached him with the idea during one of his periodic hospital stays. "Israel called me from the hospital and basically told me he wanted to go on his own. I told him, 'Get real.' But he was serious, so I went to see him. He said, 'I want to make some of my own decisions, and I want you to help me make those decisions. I know you have history; I know you can help me.' He said he just couldn't do it anymore.

Facing Future, *Israel Kamakawiwoʻole's debut departure album from the Mākaha Sons of Niʻihau, established him as a larger-than-life Island music superstar.*

A member of the Mākaha Sons for 17 years, "Bruddah Iz" eventually chafed under the strictures of the group's time-tested, traditional style.

strictures of the established Mākaha Sons of Niʻihau style. Band leader Moon Kauakahi recalled the recording sessions for that last album: "Israel tried introducing reggae and all this other stuff, and I just went, 'Nope!' A lot of groups start off playing traditional Hawaiian music, and then they go into other areas, but it's harder to come back, because the public identifies you with a certain type of music. I didn't want that to happen. He would try and put in this spark, and I would *snuff* that spark out," said Kauakahi, making a blowing sound. "I would shake my head, and he would go, 'Oh, well.'"

Israel got his chance to play reggae on *Facing Future*, most notably with the brassy "Maui Hawaiian Sup'pa Man," but most of the album sticks with the Mākaha Sons' traditional Hawaiian sound, only quieter and more simple. His contemplative take on "White Sandy Beach," a popular song from *Hoʻoluana*, highlighted Israel's new direction.

De Mello said his goal while recording Israel was to facilitate his creative flow, and so he established a flexible schedule that would allow Israel to record whenever he wanted.

One of the most famous tracks on the album, a medley of "Somewhere over the Rainbow" and "What a Wonderful World," was recorded during one of these impromptu sessions.

"One night, he was having trouble sleeping," de Mello said. "He was on oxygen and couldn't sleep well. So he'd roll over and grab his ʻukulele and start playing

"The trouble with a big band is that the paycheck gets split up. It's hard to create a living on that. He had made 11 albums with them, and for 17 years he had been on welfare. That's basically what he told me in that room."

It wasn't just about financial security, though. Israel had been chafing under the it. So about two in the morning, he calls me up and says, 'I want to record.' I told him, '20 minutes, see you there.' Now he had done that song before, on another album, but he had never done it simple with just his *'ukulele*. That night, he did four or five songs. First takes. He'd sit down and start playing, and if you weren't ready, you missed it. But we were ready."

In addition to late-night recording sessions, de Mello assigned a studio technician solely to record Israel every moment he was in the studio. "As soon as Israel's car was turned off in the parking lot, I would say, push that red button," said de Mello. "I want to hear the door opening, I want to hear this man walking across the room and sitting down in the chair."

The obsessive procedures paid off – Israel's moving spoken segments on "Hawai'i '78 Introduction" were collected from these "off time" studio recordings. When he declares, "I feel free now," it's not a scripted sentiment.

The album is full of simple moments like this; Israel was at his best when stripped to his essentials – just his delicate voice and his *'ukulele* floating alone, making it impossible to believe he could be anything other than a star.

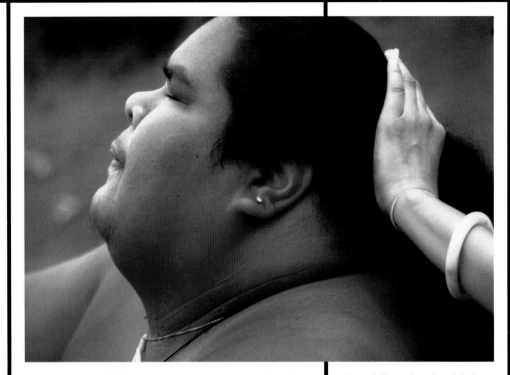

Israel Kamakawiwo'ole's simple style, delicate voice and unique vision all came together in **Facing Future,** *the breakout album certified as Hawai'i's first-ever gold record.*

10

KALAPANA
Kalapana, 1975

- *Going Going Gone*
- *The Hurt*
- *Nightbird*
- *What Do I Do*

- *To Be True*
- *When the Morning Comes*
- *Naturally*

- *All I Want*
- *Kona Daze*
- *You Make It Hard*
- *Everything Is Love*

Nothing brings back the feel of the Islands in the 1970s better than Kalapana's self-titled debut. The pure, soulful voices of Malani Bilyeu and Mackey Feary – combined with the versatility of musicians D.J. Pratt and Kirk Thompson – captured the angst, intensity and playfulness of young men coming of age in the Islands.

In a way, Kalapana was something of a "boy band," assembled specifically for their hit-making potential. In 1973, Ed Guy of Kahuku Productions, who had overseen the success of Cecilio & Kapono, was looking to assemble a larger group with that same magical C&K chemistry.

With the help of Henry Kapono, he went around town scouting talent and picked four promising candidates: Pratt and Thompson were playing together in a band called Sunlight, and Malani was playing in a little pizza place at Koko Marina. Feary, just 16, was making a name for himself as a singer/songwriter, and had opened up several times for Cecilio & Kapono. Once they played together, the band just clicked.

Of course, they still needed a name. Bilyeu described the creative selection process: "We blindfolded D.J. and did the tail-on-the-donkey thing. He picked Kalapana from the Big Island on the map. It was a pretty unknown place in those days, and there was a nice ring to it, so we went with Kalapana."

As it turned out, the name wasn't completely random – years later, Senator Spark Matsunaga told the group that it could be translated as "free beat of music."

Kahuku Productions put the members of Kalapana through an intensive training program.

"They groomed us with daily drills of guitar practice and vocal teachers. It was like going to musical college," remembered Bilyeu. The group honed their smooth sound – and built their fan base – at Toppe ada Shoppe, a club built especially for them above a clothing store on the corner of Kapi'olani and Ke'eaumoku.

In 1975, Kalapana released their eponymous debut and quickly became one of the most popular groups in Hawai'i's history. A year later, they played for more than 40,000 fans at Aloha Stadium during a concert with Cecilio & Kapono.

The songs from this debut have remained mainstays of local radio. "This music still sounds good today," said longtime record producer Tom Moffatt. "If you heard 'Naturally' or 'Nightbird' today for the first time, you would still go, 'Wow.'"

One of Hawai'i's most popular musical groups, Kalapana was initially created as a kind of Island "boy band." Left to right: Malani Bilyeu, Mackey Feary, D.J. Pratt and Kirk Thompson.

11

PARTY HULAS
Genoa Keawe, 1965

- Noho Paipai
- 'Ahulili
- Papālina Lahilahi
- Ka 'Ano'i
- Mauna Loa
- Ku'u Lei Hōkū
- Hula O Makee
- 'Alika
- Na Ka Pueo
- Green Rose
- Kane'ohe
- Ua Nani Moloka'i

Auntie Genoa Keawe is one of Hawai'i's most revered artists, and *Party Hulas*, with her signature tune "Alika," is generally regarded as her finest work. The album features an all-star backing lineup, with legends-in-their-own right Vickie I'i Rodrigues, Pauline Kekahuna, Violet Pahu Liliko'i and Benny Rogers, a crew Keawe affectionately called "the old timers."

Party Hulas was primarily intended as a resource for hula instructors, to give the correct lyrics and meaning for the most popular "war horses" of the hula canon, but producer Don McDiarmid, Jr., had a second goal in mind as well: "I started out to build a party," he explained. "When the music is good and all of a sudden some gal jumps up and starts dancing hula, now I know I got a good party. That's what I was after."

Judging from the album's steady sales since its 1965 release, McDiarmid and Keawe more than succeeded. Radio personality Honolulu Skylark said, "If you were having a lū'au, all you had to do was throw on that record. It made the party."

That *Party Hulas* made a perfect pa'ina soundtrack wasn't a complete surprise to Keawe, who said she was always mindful of the potential audience. "I tried to keep it as popular as I can with my singing. You pick up the tempo and then you slow it down, and then pick up the tempo and slow it down. You don't do all fast, you change the tempo for variety."

For those actually interested in the album's instructional aspect, Jean Sullivan provided exemplary liner notes, with tech-

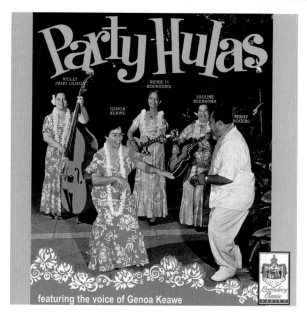

nical instructions for hula dancers as well as Hawaiian song lyrics, English translations and explanations of the *kaona* (hidden meaning) of the songs.

It's good to know, for example, that the poetic-sounding line, "A he pua 'oe ua 'ako 'ia" in "Papālina Lahilahi" actually means "You're a flower already plucked."

Keawe, still performing in her eighties, said she had no plans for retirement: "Everybody asks me, says, 'Gee, Auntie Genoa, looks like Hawaiian music is leaving us. People are not singing it too much.' I say well, as long as I'm alive, there will always be."

A later version of the album cover omitted the copy bar on the right (opposite page), which introduced the musicians and dancers in sometimes tongue-in-cheek fashion: "No, Benny's not wearing leis of orange ping-pong balls."

12

LIKE A SEABIRD IN THE WIND
Olomana, 1976

- The Lion
- Ku'u Home O Kahaluu
- Home
- Grandfather's Music
- Ku'u Lei Awapuhi
- O Malia
- So Free
- Seabird
- Lullabye

Jerry Santos and Robert Beaumont were among the leaders of the Hawaiian Renaissance, creating both Hawaiian- and English-language songs with polished production values.

KCCN general manager Mike Kelly, who worked with Olomana on their debut, said, "What set them apart was the tunings they used; they combined slack key with regular tunings, and they blended the traditional and the contemporary together so beautifully." Santos' "Ku'u Home O Kahalu'u" was one of the biggest hits off the album.

Olomana's intention was that *Like a Seabird* be a local version of a rock opera, with a cohesive feel for each side. According to Santos, "The songs, taken in context, create a storyline. It was intended to be a social, cultural and political statement about our Island home, her people and the changes that we were facing."

Although the equipment in engineer Jim Linkner's studio was hardly state of the art – the album was recorded onto an eight-track machine – Olomana overcame technical limitations by spending more than 400 hours in the studio, perfecting their sound and coming up with creative workarounds. To capture the wave sounds, for example, the crew actually drove to the beach one night with a battery-operated tape recorder.

"When you record the ocean, even if there's big surf, all it sounds like is sshshshsh, just a hissing sound," Linkner remembered. "So what we did was, at Kāhala Beach Park, there's a ditch that drains into the ocean, but when the tide is coming up, the ocean runs into the drainage ditch. So the wave would wash along the ditch, and we would run alongside with the microphone dangling down."

The resulting album was a masterpiece that, along with the Beamer brothers' *Honolulu City Lights*, brought Hawaiian music to new heights of production and feeling.

In an interview for the 1978 book *Da Kine Sound*, Beaumont described how he came up with the album title: "I was sitting on a rock on Magic Island near Ala Moana watching these guys fishing. These two birds came by flying in unison. My first idea was, *Like seabirds in the wind*. Which has a lot to do with our music. I mean, we flow together when we play. That's what it is, a flow."

Olomana spent more than 400 hours in Jim Linkner's studio to record Like a Seabird in the Wind. *Left to right: Robert Beaumont, Jim Linkner (seated), Liko Martin and Jerry Santos.*

13

R.S.V.P.
The Invitations, 1959

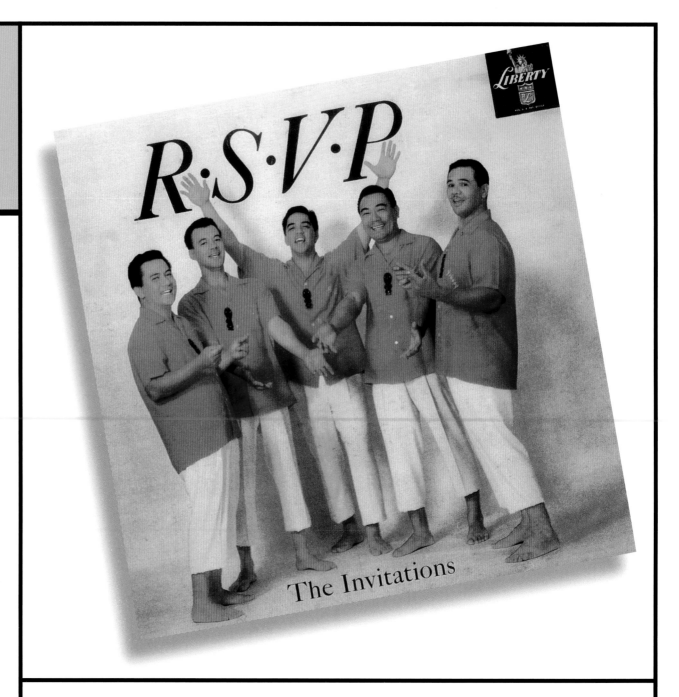

- Nani Waimea
- Pretty Red Hibiscus
- Ka Makani Kaili Aloha
- Mr. Wonderful
- Hawaiian Hospitality
- Invitation
- Sweet Someone
- Princess Poo-poo-ly
- Hawaii Calls
- Susie Anna E
- Mauna Loa
- Lei Aloha, Lei Makamae

Since 1999, radio host Harry B. Soria, Jr., has dedicated at least one of his *Territorial Airwaves* shows every year to the music of The Invitations. Aside from the group's enduring popularity, there's another reason Soria established this annual ritual: most of The Invitations' recordings, including *RSVP*, are out of print.

"I'll play The Invitations special on my show, and the calls come, 'Where can I get that?' Soria said. "As soon as my show finishes, the last few bars play, I'll get 25 phone calls before I leave the studio.

Now when I start the show, I say, 'Push *record* on your tape recorder now. Make yourself a home copy. That's all you can do.'

It's been decades since The Invitations recorded *RSVP*, their debut album. The fact that listeners still request their music is a testament to the lasting impact of the group, which consisted of Buddy Fo, Johnny Costello, Sonny Kamaka and Clem Low.

"They sang Hawaiian songs, done in Hollywood style and done really well," said Byron Yasui, a professor of music at the University of Hawai'i. "Not many people can sing how they did, because it's so challenging.

The original Invitations pose backstage at the Korean Village in the International Marketplace. Left to right: Buddy Fo, Clem Low, Sonny Kamaka and Johnny Costello. Opposite: An early fifth member of the group, Alex Kaeck, appears on the cover of R.S.V.P.

They were incredible vocalists and musicians, and they deserve all the recognition they can get."

In 1960 the Invitations followed R.S.V.P. with a second Liberty Records album, this one recorded with Billy May and his Orchestra.

The story of The Invitations starts with another group, the Richard Kauhi Quartette. The group included Kamaka, Costello, Jimmy Kaku and, of course, Kauhi, whose jazz influences made him one of the pioneers of contemporary Hawaiian music.

In the 1950s, the Quartette elevated four-part harmony to a new level. Fo, a teenager at the time, was a fan, sometimes cutting class to watch the band perform.

"Richard was the happening thing," Fo remembered. "It really inspired me to not get into *traditional* Hawaiian music, which was all around me all the time. My father and my sister were both Hawaiian entertainers. I wanted to do something else."

The Quartette eventually disbanded, with Kauhi embarking on a solo career in Palm Springs. Fo became a beach boy in Waikīkī, where Kamaka also worked, and the two became roommates, sharing a small studio apartment near Kūhiō Beach. When not giving surfing lessons, they jammed together on the beach – Fo with his percussion and Kamaka on his guitar.

"I told Sonny I wanted to put a group together, but I didn't want it to sound like what he did with Richard," Fo said. "We needed to have a very unique sound. I wanted it to be different."

The jazzy, four-part harmony groups of the '50s heavily influenced Fo. He and Kamaka frequented the Waikiki Tavern, just to hear whatever was playing on the club's jukebox. They usually didn't have much money in their pockets, so they wound up asking other customers to play songs they wanted to hear.

"When Sonny heard the Four Freshmen, he goes, 'Oh, wow, that sounds great.' I said, 'We need to go in that direction,'" Fo recalled. "Then we got ahold of a record by the Hi-Los. A lot of our inspiration came from two haole groups in the Mainland."

The next step was finding two more musicians to complete their own foursome. This took some manipulation on Fo's part. Both he and Kamaka agreed that Costello, another Richard Kauhi Quartette alum, was a great bassist. But there was a hitch: since the Quartette had broken up, Costello and Kamaka hadn't been on speaking terms. That didn't deter Fo, though. He decided to recruit Costello anyway.

"I went up to Johnny's house in Kapahulu, and I see this guy cleaning a car in the driveway," Fo reminisced. "He goes, 'Whatchu like?' I said, 'Me and Sonny like you come play with us.' He said, 'I no like play with Sonny.' I tell him, 'Bruddah, he really *aloha* you, you know. You should come Kūhiō Beach."

Fo gave Kamaka a similar story, telling him that Costello really missed him. It worked. When Kamaka and Costello got together, they quickly settled their differences. They just needed to recruit one more vocalist. They decided on pianist Clem Low.

Low was skeptical about joining at first. Until he heard Fo, Kamaka and Costello sing their three-part arrangement of "Ka Makani Kaili Aloha," that is. Then he immediately agreed to join.

"That was the beginning of The Invitations," Fo said. "We went to Liberty House and bought matching white pants and red shirts and had our names embroidered on them. And we'd jump in my old '36 Ford my mother gave me – the kine you need to push to start – and we'd practice every day for hours, while we drove up and down Kalākaua Avenue. Everybody in the car was hot, but we rolled up the windows to hear the harmonies. We learned how to blend."

The Invitations started playing for free at the International Marketplace. When they started packing in the crowds, Waikīkī entertainer Martin Denny, who played at Don the Beachcomber's next door, took notice.

Denny set up a meeting between The Invitations and executives at Liberty Records. The group impressed the "suits" from New York with their distinct blend of Hawaiian music, jazz and four-part harmo-

ny. Liberty signed them immediately, making The Invitations one of the first local acts to sign with that label.

In Hollywood, the group was backed by the famed Russ Garcia orchestra, which included legendary musicians such as Barney Kessel and Laurindo Almeida. Those sessions produced such classics as "Sweet Someone" and "Susie Anna E."

The Invitations perform onstage at the Korean Village, after Clem Low's departure from the group. Left to right: Buddy Fo, Johnny Costello, Sonny Kamaka and Alec Among.

"It was an overwhelming experience – these guys were so pro," Fo said. "When the cellist started playing 'Ka Makani Kaili Aloha,' we couldn't even sing; the tears started to roll down our eyes. But after we got through, we knew we did well. Those guys told us, 'You folks sang so well.' For young punks who came off the beach in Waikīkī, it was such an honor to hear that."

14

MUSIC OF HAWAI'I
Jack de Mello, 1965

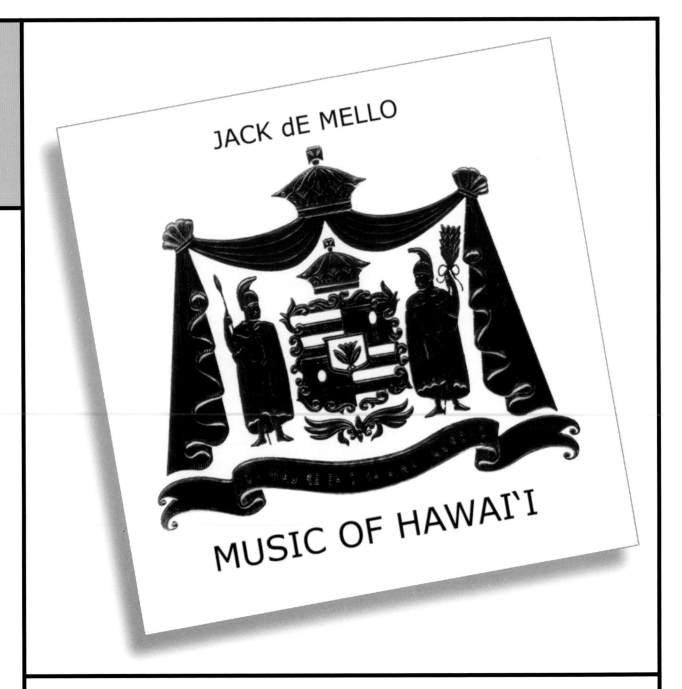

JACK dE MELLO

MUSIC OF HAWAI'I

- *Hawai'i Pono'i*
- *Ku'u Ipo I Ka He'e Pue One*
- *Song of the Sea*
- *My Hawai'i*
- *Hawaiian War Chant*
- *Beyond the Reef*

- *Waikīkī*
- *Dancing Breeze*
- *Nani Wale Lihu'e*
- *Kamehameha Waltz*
- *Kalua*
- *A'oia*
- *Mutiny on the Bounty*
- *Pūpū 'O Ni'ihau*

- *Across the Sea*
- *Aloha Nō Au I Ko Maka*
- *Sea Dreams*
- *Liholiho*
- *Tiny Bubbles*
- *The Hilo March*

- *Diamond Head*
- *Ke Kali Nei Au*
- *Valley of the Orchids*
- *I Am Hawai'i*
- *Nani Ke Li'i Ki'eki'e*
- *Hawai'i Aloha*
- *Aloha 'Oe*

Hawaiian music is an adaptable genre – over the past 50 years, the art form has stretched to accommodate rock, jazz, lounge and reggae, all without losing its essential quality. Even considering all these stylistic excursions, though, it has to be said that no one has successfully stretched Hawaiian music farther than Jack de Mello.

For his acclaimed six-part *Music of Hawai'i* anthology, de Mello tackled some of Hawai'i's most popular songs from a 140-year period and gave them an epic treatment, using an 80-piece orchestra and choir to re-imagine old standards as high-budget extravaganzas.

"I took Hawaiian music a few steps beyond what I heard when I first got there in 1947," said de Mello. "Then, it was all the standard two guitars, a *'ukulele* and an acoustic bass, and people singing. My feeling about the music I heard during those years was that it was a heck of a lot better than people thought it was. So I thought I would take it to the extreme dimension."

De Mello was something of a musical prodigy: as a six-year-old, he was already playing the trumpet in front of audiences. His son, Jon de Mello, said his father even traded lessons with the famed composer Igor Stravinsky when he was 11.

"He got a call from Igor Stravinsky, and Igor wanted to learn about how a marching band worked," Jon said. "My father wanted to know how to write for a big orchestra, on the classical side of things. So they traded a dozen lessons or so and went back and forth. Stravinsky, at the top of the manuscript pages every time they would have a lesson, would write, 'constancy of purpose.' Stravinsky was trying to show him the continuity of things."

Although Jack de Mello was born and raised in California, he did have family ties to Hawai'i. His grandfather, originally from the Azores, immigrated to the Big Island in 1878. Jack's father then moved to California, but he and his wife would tell their son stories of Hawai'i.

So when the management of the Royal Hawaiian Hotel invited de Mello and his band to play at the hotel's 1947, post-war reopening on O'ahu, he jumped at the chance.

At the time, he was working as the musical director of NBC Radio in San Francisco, but when he heard the Hawaiian music being played all over Waikīkī, opportunity flashed for de Mello. Here was a brand-new area of music that he could make his mark on.

Jack de Mello conducts during a recording session with the London Symphony.

In January 1947, Jack de Mello, Joe Reichman and their 18-piece orchestra arrive from San Francisco for a three-month engagement at the Royal Hawaiian Hotel's Monarch Room. Standing: Clara Inter (Hilo Hattie), left, Joe Reichman, fifth from right, Jack and Penelope de Mello, sixth and seventh from right, and vocalist Lei Becker, eighth from right. Kneeling: The musicians and dancers of Al Kealoha Perry's troupe.

"I just saw all of the wonderful things that could happen with the music of Hawai'i," de Mello recalled.

After returning to the Mainland for three months to wrap up his commitments, de Mello moved to O'ahu and founded his own record label, Aloha Record Co., later renamed Music of Polynesia. The first song he recorded under the label, "Coconut Willie," was an immediate success, although de Mello did encounter one hitch: "I remember getting the first order of 5,000 '78s shipped over on Matson, and they all warped. They looked like waffles. We had to toss them all. But I learned from that."

Music of Polynesia released a variety of Hawaiian and Pacific-Islander music during the '50s and early '60s, but it was the *Music*

of Hawaii series that really made de Mello's name. Releasing a project of such "extreme dimensions" was a gamble – no one had ever done a completely symphonic interpretation of Hawaiian music, so the waters were untested.

As it turned out, there were no recording studios in Hawai'i big enough for de Mello's vision – he had to go to London. Luckily he had friends in high places: Henry Mancini found him a contractor there named Sydney Sax who could get him musicians from the London Symphony.

De Mello would compose all his music in Hawai'i, then send the scores to London, where they were copied and the individual instruments parts were extracted prior to his arrival. When this was completed, de Mello could begin working.

"I'd fly over and stand outside the studio with Sydney and ask him a simple question: 'Did everyone show up, Sydney?' And he would say, 'Of course.' We would walk in through the door, and here were 70 or 80 of the finest European musicians. Hell of a thrill."

Of course, 80 of Europe's finest musicians don't come cheap. Jon de Mello, who accompanied his father on several London trips, said a single day of orchestral recording at Decca Studios cost about $80,000. As a result, just 23 minutes was allotted for each song. "We'd have three chances to record it," said Jon. "We debugged during the first pass and the second time was usually the take we used. Sometimes we did a third, but that was it."

Jack de Mello takes a break during a London recording session with Nina Kealiiwahamana and her mother-in-law, Christine Rapozo.

Adding to the complicated procedure was the fact that de Mello didn't have the luxury of multi-track recording or overdubbing; the entire orchestra had to play at once, with no mistakes. Musicians were spread throughout the enormous studio, with baffles to prevent sound bleed between sections, and technicians were assigned just to anticipate which sections would need emphasis at any given time.

Jon said, "They'd have an orchestrator in the engineering booth calling it out as it would come, saying, 'Okay, here comes the flute solo, two, three,' and they'd push the fader. 'Okay, push it up and then fade it back down.' The recording process was an absolute performance."

The first anthology, *Music of Hawai'i: Missionaries to Statehood*, was recorded in five three-hour sessions on Oct. 25, 26 and 27 of 1965, and it became an immediate success – so much so that Ala Moana Center sponsored the rest of the series, which continued chronologically from statehood until the (then) present day. De Mello has produced all kinds of music since that project, including children's music, television themes and Japanese music, but *Music of Hawai'i* remains his most beloved work.

15

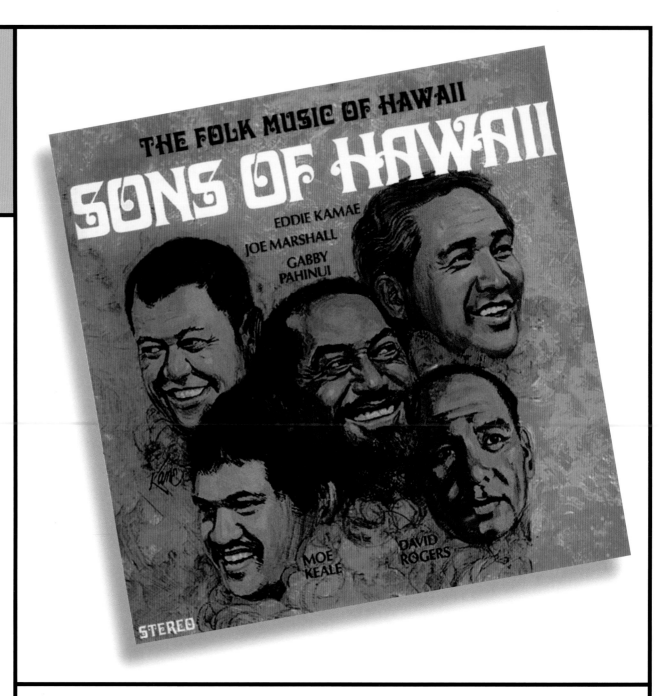

THE FOLK MUSIC OF HAWAII
Sons of Hawaii, 1971

- *No Ke Ano Ahiahi*
- *Kanaka Waiwai*
- *Ku'u Pete*
- *Mauna Alani*
- *Waikīkī Hula*
- *Ka Lae O Ka'ena*
- *Hanohano Hawai'i*
- *I Love Chritmas*
- *Po'e Koa*
- *Moe Kokolo*
- *Huelo*
- *Wai Ulu*
- *Manu Kapalulu*
- *Aloha Chant*

The Sons of Hawaii formed in the 1960s, a group that included some of the Islands' finest musicians: bassist Joe Marshall, steel guitarist David "Feet" Rogers, 'ukulele virtuoso Eddie Kamae and slack-key icon Gabby Pahinui. With their lively performances and indisputable musicianship, they quickly lured crowds to their unpredictable shows at The Sandbox, a nightclub in the Sand Island industrial area.

But after recording a handful of albums with Hula Records, the fast-fingered, hard-living members disbanded, opting to follow solo career paths instead.

It wasn't until 1971 that the Sons of Hawaii reunited, thanks to the persuasive skills of three young men who owned a fledgling record label known as Panini Records. *Sons of Hawaii*, also known as *The Folk Music of Hawaii*, marked the group's re-entry into the local music scene after an eight-year hiatus.

Hawai'i was more than happy to welcome them back. The album also featured 'ukulele master and vocalist Moe Keale, making his debut as the fifth member of the Sons. To understand the significance of this album, however, it's important to start from the beginning.

The beginning for group founder Eddie Kamae started with an old 'ukulele his older brother found on a city bus and brought home. Kamae tinkered with the instrument, figuring out by himself how to mimic the songs he heard on the radio. The songs weren't Hawaiian, but Spanish, and Kamae enjoyed their exotic rhythms. He got so good at playing that he started performing wherever

he could, at Charlie's Taxi stand, near storefronts or movie theaters.

"My father used to take me to all my gigs, and I knew in his heart, he was proud of me," Kamae said. "He asked me once to play Hawaiian music – he loved Hawaiian music – and I said, 'Nah, it's too easy.' My father never said anything about it again. It wasn't till he died that I realized this was the only thing he had ever asked of me."

That memory stayed with Kamae, even years later, when he drove out to Waimānalo to visit some friends. When he arrived at their home, he found them caring for their friend. It was Gabby Pahinui, a musician Kamae had met before, who was ill and unable to swallow his food.

"Gabby told me, 'Son, go get your 'ukulele," Kamae said. "I had it in my car. Although Gabby couldn't eat or sing, he could still play his guitar. We played together, and I loved the sound of it."

Group founder Eddie Kamae: *"There isn't any way to really describe those days. It was like a guy who searches all his life for something, and suddenly, there it is."*

Kamae's life would never be the same. He stayed with Pahinui for one day, then two, then three. Those days turned into a month, then another. Pahinui's friend, bassist Joe Marshall, dropped by, eventually joining in on their impromptu jam sessions. For Kamae, the combination just felt right.

"There isn't any way to really describe those days," Kamae once said. "It was like a guy who searches all his life for something, and suddenly, there it is."

The Sons of Hawaii were born. The three musicians decided to recruit another member to round out the band, one who could play steel guitar as well as Pahinui. It was Marshall who suggested David "Feet" Rogers, a crackerjack on steel guitar, much like his father George and uncle Benny.

"Feet was very reserved, but if he loved something, he'd tell you," Kamae said. "When we'd get through a session, he'd say, 'Pretty song.' That's all I'd hear from him. He had great technique, though. I loved that beautiful sound of his steel."

During that time, Kamae dug up some Hawaiian songbooks by Johnny Noble and Charles King which helped to deepen his newfound appreciation of the beauty and complexity of Hawaiian music. These books made him want to learn more about his heritage.

Kamae sought out Mary Kawena Pukui, a master of the Hawaiian language at the Bishop Museum. With her help he unearthed several old songbooks, full of Hawaiian songs that had never been recorded. Other songs had simply been forgotten over time. The Sons resurrected many of these songs on the albums they recorded with Hula Records, arranging them in their own distinctive contemporary Hawaiian style.

In the mid-'60s, however, the four members decided to part ways, for a number of reasons. For several years Pahinui, Kamae, Marshall and Rogers played on their own or partnered with other musicians, never quite achieving the kind of chemistry that bound the Sons of Hawaii together.

In 1970, Steve Siegfried, Witt Shingle and Lawrence Brown – all just a few years out of high school – made it their mission to bring back the kind of Hawaiian music they'd grown up with – the music of Gabby Pahinui and the Sons of Hawaii.

It wasn't easy to reunite the legendary band. Somehow, though, they convinced Kamae, and he helped them draw the other three members in. Kamae even managed to persuade Rogers, a merchant marine, to jump ship for the reunion.

"It was hard," Siegfried said. "Everyone was reticent. They hadn't played together in years. Gabby had stopped recording completely. No one knew what to expect."

But when they got together, the magic was still there, just as fresh as it had been years before. Kamae insisted on adding one more musician to the mix, Moe Keale.

"Moe was playing at Trader Vic's – it used to be where TGIF is now on King Street," Kamae explained. "He had a voice that was so special. When I asked if he could join us, he just said, 'Can I start now?'"

Kamae, as he was known to do, resurrected several traditional Hawaiian songs that had all but disappeared with time. The Sons reintroduced Hawai'i to the ancient song "No Ke Ano Ahiahi." It became one of the Islands' best-known songs, conventionally performed the same way Kamae arranged it decades ago. The album also featured one of the first recordings of "Kanaka Waiwai." Keale, who discovered the song on a trip to his family's home on Ni'ihau, sang lead vocals.

Sons of Hawaii was Panini Records' first album, and its producers made sure they did it right, holding frequent rehearsals, allowing ample recording time, employing high-quality engineering and packaging the album with impressive liner notes and a companion booklet on Hawaiian music. The release celebrated the return of the Sons of Hawaii in style.

The album is widely considered the Sons of Hawaii's masterpiece, one unlike anything Islanders had ever heard. This was one of the albums that fueled the Hawaiian Renaissance of the 1970s, a cultural movement that rekin-

dled interest in Hawaiian music. Alongside groups such as The Sunday Manoa, the Sons of Hawaii became pioneers of the contemporary Hawaiian sound.

"Those were just joyous, joyous times," Kamae remembered. "For us and for Hawaiian music."

The Sons of Hawaii brought together some of Hawai'i's finest musicians: steel guitarist David "Feet" Rogers (left), bassist Joe Marshall (left, below) and, opposite, left to right, Moe Keale and Gabby Pahinui.

16

THE BEST OF ALFRED APAKA
Alfred Apaka, 1960

THE BEST OF ALFRED APAKA
With THE HAWAIIAN VILLAGE SERENADERS

- Song Of The Islands (Na Lei O Hawaii)
- Lovely Hula Hands
- My Isle Of Golden Dreams
- The Hukilau Song
- Beyond The Reef
- The Moon of Manakoora

- The Hawaiian Wedding Song
- Little Brown Gal
- Sleepy Lagoon
- I Will Remember You
- Hapa-Haole Hula Girl
- Aloha Oe
- Ebb Tide

- You Are Beautiful
- Princess Poo-poo-ly Has Plenty Papaya
- Forevermore
- Old Plantation
- Far Across The Sea
- Legend Of The Rain

- The Song Of Love (Da Hill Sigh Oh/Dahil Sa Lyo)
- The Magic Islands
- Hawaiian Love Call
- Bali Ha'i
- Flowers Of Paradise
- I Wish They Didn't Mean Goodbye

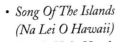

Alfred Apaka was the ultimate performer, handsome and charismatic, with an amazingly smooth and potent baritone. In the years after the Second World War, Apaka became the foremost icon of hapa-haole music, spreading aloha both in Hawai'i and on the Mainland in his signature costume – a white sharkskin suit and a lei of sweet red Maui carnations.

At a 1997 celebration of his legacy, *kupuna* Gladys A. Brandt told the crowd that the beach boys of Waikīkī thanked Apaka every day for the romances inspired by his ballads. "One can imagine the scene," she said. "Quiet waves, a moonlit night, a soft warm breeze and the song, 'Beyond the Reef.' Who could resist a strong, dark-eyed Hawaiian sea god under such circumstances – especially if a mai tai or two had been part of the evening?"

Alfred's father was also a singer, although it wasn't his main profession. Alfred Aiu Afat Sr. served five terms in the Territorial Legislature. Alfred's family name at birth was also Afat. But while he was in high school, his father's sister adopted a Hawaiian transliteration of the name in order to gain admission to San Francisco Nursing School, which at that time took only a small number of Chinese students. Alfred took the new Hawaiian handle as his stage name and later had his name legally changed.

Apaka's vocal talents emerged during his last year of high school. Roosevelt High School established an *a cappella* choir in 1938, under the direction of one Hedwig Finkenbinder. Don McDiarmid, Jr., of Hula

Records was at the signups, and he recalled the scene: "Something like 300 kids showed up, and she whittled it down to 150. After she got those, she did auditions for soloists, and Alfred was the one picked for males."

McDiarmid went home and over dinner told his father about Alfred's amazing voice. Don McDiarmid, Sr., happened to be the director of the Royal Hawaiian Hotel Orchestra, which was at that time looking for a new singer.

Don McDiarmid, Jr., remembered he convinced Alfred to come down to his father's auditions. "Alfred got up first and sang one song, and my dad turned and told everybody else, 'OK, fine, that's the guy I want. That's the end of that. You boys go

In 1955 Henry J. Kaiser hired Alfred to headline in the Tapa Room in Kaiser's new Hawaiian Village Hotel in Waikīkī.

home; thank you very much for coming.'"

It was the start of a steady rise to fame. Alfred Apaka immediately began working six nights a week with McDiarmid's orchestra (he was onstage at his own Roosevelt High School graduation party), and soon he attracted the attention of Ray Kinney, an orchestra leader who played the Hawaiian Room at the Hotel Lexington in New York City.

Alfred Apaka spread aloha *around the world in his signature outfit of a white sharkskin suit and red Maui carnation* lei.

Kinney hired Apaka as his lead vocalist and flew him to New York in 1940. Alfred's flexible voice allowed him to easily accommodate Kinney's tenor arrangements, and he soon earned a name for himself among the socialites as the "darling of Manhattan."

After appearing in the long-running

Broadway musical *Hellzapoppin'*, Apaka returned to Hawai'i in 1943. World War II was in full swing by this time, but Apaka's flat feet prevented him from serving, so he assembled his own band and became a fixture at Jimmy Walker's La Hula Rhumba until 1947.

He then jumped at an opportunity to perform with the house band of the *Hawai'i Calls* radio show, which was broadcast across the nation.

Apaka had recorded songs before with various labels, but his rising profile during this period led to a marked increase in recordings. He cut records with the Bell Record Company, radio personality J. "Akuhead" Pupule's Aku Records and also with Decca.

In 1952, Bob Hope caught his act at the Beachcomber in Waikīkī and immediately brought him to Los Angeles to appear on both his television and his radio show. Hope also found Apaka an agent, Buddy Taub. Apaka, his wife Edna Blake, and his young son Jeffrey lived in Beverly Hills for a few years. He traveled extensively, performing across the United States, and also landed bit parts in several Paramount Studios films.

His career got a further boost when Henry Kaiser took him under his wing in 1955 and set him up in the Tapa Room in the brand-new Kaiser Hawaiian Village Hotel. Apaka's son Jeff said Kaiser used his extensive connections to promote Alfred. "Henry Kaiser respected my father like his son and right-hand man," Jeff explained. "Henry was the one who put him on *Ed*

Near Queen's Surf in 1951, Alfred poses with the Hula Nani dancers during the filming of a television special.

Sullivan and *Dinah Shore, Jack Parr,* Coca Cola specials."

In fact, in January of 1960, Apaka was granted a sponsorship for a national TV pilot in which he held the starring role. The world seemed to be his for the taking. It was a cruel shock, then, when Apaka collapsed on a paddleball court at the Central Y.M.C.A. in Honolulu on Jan. 30. Alfred Apaka was only 40 years old when he died, seemingly at the peak of both his health and his career.

The greatest hits compilation that Decca released later that year had already been in production when Apaka died.

According to the album notes, "The recordings in this album were not originally intended as a memorial. These, Alfred Apaka's last recorded performances, were to be a tribute to the man in his lifetime. *The Best of Alfred Apaka* was to be a promise of more to come."

17

THE DON HO SHOW!
Don Ho, 1965

- Night Life
- E Lei Ka Lei Lei (Beach Party Song)
- I'll Remember You
- A Taste of Honey
- My Hawaiian Song of Love
- Pearly Shells

- La Bamba
- Blue Coral
- Hawaiian Wedding Song
- Waikiki
- Nini Waimea
- Night Life – (Reprise)
- Lover's Prayer

- Lahaina Luna
- Ain't No Big Thing
- The Following Sea
- Sweet Someone
- If I Had To Do It Over Again
- You May Go
- Maka Hilahila

- Suck 'Em Up
- You Are Beautiful
- Hang On Sloopy
- I Wish They Didn't Mean Goodbye
- Night Life

Hawai'i has produced no bigger star than Don Ho, a living legend known for his chiseled features, languorous charm and sleepy baritone voice. This album is recorded live at Duke Kahanamoku's and released by Reprise Records.

Apart from Israel Kamakawiwo'ole, no Hawai'i musician has achieved more widespread recognition than Ho. In the 1960s he became a household name, with catchy, self-indulgent tunes such as "Tiny Bubbles" and "Suck 'Em Up" and plaintive, wistful numbers such as "I'll Remember You."

But Ho is more than a musician. He is an entertainer in the truest sense of the word.

He knows how to engage a crowd – rousing them to clap along with his songs or laugh at his stories. During shows, Ho often coaxes audience members onto the stage for a hug or a kiss. It is his easygoing style that has attracted a legion of loyal fans, many who have returned to see Ho perform in Waikīkī for decades.

"Unpredictable, that's how Kimo McVay used to introduce him when he played at Duke's – 'The Unpredictable Don Ho,'" said veteran promoter Tom Moffatt. "It was never the same show; you never knew what going to happen. Everybody was looking for the new Alfred Apaka, and this guy was the opposite – he'd be at his organ, always with a drink in his hand. He could end up playing till three in the morning."

Perhaps there's no other entertainer more associated with Waikīkī than Ho. But he actually grew

With trademark drink in hand, Don Ho held court behind the organ at Duke Kahanamoku's, where he recorded The Don Ho Show! *in 1965.*

up a country boy in Kāneʻohe. During his childhood, taro patches carpeted much of the young town. There were few houses. And the Pali tunnel, which now connects Windward Oʻahu to the Honolulu area, had yet to be built.

"Kāneʻohe was so much of an impact on me as a child, and after I served in the military, I just wanted to come home and settle there forever," said Ho.

Backed by the multi-talented Aliis, Ho's freewheeling shows and best-selling albums helped make him an international icon.

After serving in the U.S. Air Force, Ho took over his mother's Kāneʻohe cocktail lounge, Honey's (it was named for her). It wasn't a huge moneymaker, at first. The club was usually empty, save for some family friends who helped spread the word about the modest venue.

"One day, my dad said, 'Son, why don't you go make music?'" recalled Ho, who then recruited a few friends to start a band. "I was terrible, so I just played softly."

Nevertheless, Honey's business began to boom. The club didn't need to advertise. Customers spread the word on their own. People ventured from Waikīkī to the country venue, eager to see this magnetic entertainer perform.

People rose from their chairs to dance along with Ho's tunes. Honey's was often so crowded that customers established a unique way to catch waitresses' attention. If a customer wanted a drink, he lit a match and held it up. Ho, of course, was a smart businessman as well as an entertainer: if he spotted that customer first, he'd shout in the middle of a song, "Eh! Get that guy a drink!"

"That was a great place, whatta party!" exclaimed Hula Records producer Don McDiarmid, Jr. "It got so crowded, you couldn't even get in the door. You'd pay $500 to just sit down and watch."

Honey's became the springboard for other Hawaiʻi artists, including Marlene Sai and Nani Lee. When legendary promoter Kimo McVay convinced both Sai and Lee to leave Honey's for Duke Kahanamoku's in Waikīkī, Ho thought, *To heck with it* and decided to start his own venue in Waikīkī. He opened Honey's Waikīkī near the intersection of Liliʻuokalani and Kalākaua avenues. It was a modest establishment, with a 12-foot stage in one corner of the lounge. Ho's doorman was Kui Lee, his longtime friend who composed many of the songs in Ho's repertoire, including "I'll Remember You" and "One Paddle Two Paddle."

"We were drawing all the crowds; we were always packed before we even made records," Ho said. "We had a great following from all over the island – Hau'ula, Kalihi, wherever – who came and supported us."

Ho was popular on O'ahu, but it wasn't until he started performing at Duke's in 1962 that he became an international icon. It was the Duke himself who asked Ho to play at the famed Waikīkī supper club with him.

"One day, I see Kimo in this joint with Duke Kahanamoku, his mother, his lawyer and his bookkeeper," Ho said. "I'm sitting in the back, and Duke comes up and gives me a big, fat kiss on my lips in front of everybody and said, 'Don, I want you to come play for me.' I can't refuse. I have so much *aloha* and respect for the Duke."

Ho's show was titled "Honey's Lounge at Duke Kahanamoku's." Like every other venue Ho played, Duke's packed crowds in. The Aliis accompanied Ho with piano, drums, two guitars and xylophone, doubling on several other instruments.

The Don Ho Show! was the first of a pair of albums recorded back to back at Duke's. It featured "E Lei Ka Lei Lei," "I'll Remember You" and "Hawaiian Wedding Song." Those carefree, crazy years at Duke's propelled Ho into the national spotlight, with performances at such famed venues as Cocoanut Grove in Hollywood and the Sands in Las Vegas as well as TV appearances with Johnny Carson and Art Linkletter. He even landed his own hour-long color-TV special.

Ho became famous in the rollicking years of the '60s – an era when tiki torches abounded, mai tais flowed and Waikīkī was *the* place to be. But for decades, Ho has personified Hawai'i for the rest of the world, earning him a permanent place in American pop culture.

"I never think about how long I've been performing," Ho said. "I just think it's unfinished business, I gotta keep doing it till I get it right. Besides, that's what keeps me healthy. I really believe you should do what you love, live a good life, don't take ourselves too seriously and make people laugh a lot. And we laugh a lot."

As his wife, Nadine, looks on, a frisky Duke Kahanamoku dances hula at his namesake Waikīkī nightclub.

18

NINA
Nina Kealiiwahamana, 1978

- Ku'u Ipo I Ka He'e Pu'e One
- Moloka'i Nui A Hina
- Adios Ke Aloha
- Maunawili
- 'Akaka Falls
- Nani Wale Lihu'e
- Beyond the Reef
- Heha Waipi'o
- 'Akahi Ho'i (Thine Alone)
- Pūpū A 'O Ewa (Pearly Shells)
- Kaleleonālani
- Hilo Hanakahi
- Moloka'i Waltz (He Nani Kū Kilakila)
- E Huli Mākou
- Pūpū Ni'ihau (The Shells of Ni'ihau)
- Hawai'i Aloha

This album compiles the greatest hits of Nina Kealiiwahamana's work with Jack de Mello, and it makes it clear why she's known as one of Hawai'i's great voices.

Nina is the daughter of Vicki I'i Rodrigues, an influential figure in Hawaiian music who performed on the very first *Hawai'i Calls* radio show in 1935. Nina followed in her mother's footsteps and was a regular on *Hawai'i Calls* from 1957 until its last broadcast in 1974.

She recalled the show with affection. "We were just one big happy family," she said. "And it was like being on *Hit Parade*, because you sang all the best songs of the day."

It was here that Nina met Jack de Mello, who would go on to record some of her most beloved tunes. De Mello knew immediately after seeing her that he needed to work with her. "I went to the Moana Hotel in the early '60s to see *Hawai'i Calls* for the first time, and there were three ladies

onstage with Webley Edwards. I was amazed at what I heard, because this one young girl was a jewel."

Her warm, almost operatic soprano was a perfect match for de Mello's orchestral arrangements. Jack's son, Jon de Mello, remembered the first time she sang in front of the London studio sessions. "Nina opened her mouth to sing 'Ku'u Ipo' and the orchestra almost fell off their chairs. They didn't think this little lady was going to have a voice like that. After the take, the orchestra actually applauded."

Music from the Land of Aloha, released in 1961, was the first album, and Nina went on to work with de Mello on the *Music of Hawai'i* series (number 14 on our list).

Jon de Mello said the lasting appeal of her music comes from her heart: "Nina has been family for years; she still is. She's so gentle and warm, and when she sings, you can tell."

Below left: interviewed by Barbara Walters and framed by the Ilikai Hotel, Nina Kealiiwahamana was the first Island entertainer to appear on NBC-TV's Today Show, *in 1975. Left: Benny Kalama and Nina perform together at a 1990 concert at Keio University in Tokyo.*

19

CECILIO & KAPONO
Cecilio & Kapono, 1974

- *Feeling Just the Way I Do (Over You)*
- *Lifetime Party*
- *Sunflower*
- *Lovin' in Your Eyes*
- *All in Love Is Fair*
- *Gotta Get Away*
- *Song for Someone*
- *Friends*
- *Sunshine Love*

Cecilio Rodriguez and Henry Kapono hadn't been playing together for years when they recorded their debut album in 1974. But judging from their uncanny harmonies and feel-good, folk rock tunes, they sure sounded like it.

"We met just eight months earlier through some friends who thought Cecilio and I might make a good combo," Kapono explained. "We went up to the North Shore, played a couple songs and it just worked. The thing about us, we're always listening to each other while we're singing. That's why we were able to perform so well together."

Cecilio & Kapono landed a gig at the Rainbow Villa, attracting sold-out crowds at the Waikīkī venue. When they took their show to California, a scout from Columbia Records noticed the two playing at the Troubadour in Hollywood. The duo signed on for a three-record deal.

Their self-titled debut featured some of the top studio musicians of the time, including bassist Leland Sklar and drummer Russ Kunkel, and it produced such hits as "Lifetime Party" and "Friends."

C&K recorded eight albums together before returning to their solo careers in 1981. Today, more than two decades later, both are still known as parts of the popular duo.

"It was the '70s, and they were just so big, along with other young Hawaiian musicians like Kalapana," said promoter Tom Moffatt, who coordinated the group's first concert. "Their powerful blend of voices just grabbed everyone's attention."

People still love hearing them. In 2003, Cecilio & Kapono reunited for a "Lifetime Party – 30 Years of Friends" concert at the Waikīkī Shell, which was recorded live for a CD and DVD release.

"It amazes me that people still love our music, and that makes our lives so easy," Kapono laughed. "When we perform on stage, people practically sing the songs for us because they know all the words."

Henry Kapono (left) and Cecilio Rodriguez in the studio: "We're always listening to each other when we're singing. That's why we're able to perform so well together."

20

HAWAIʻI's MAHI BEAMER
Mahi Beamer, 1959

- Opening Chant
- Pūpū Hinu Hinu
- Nā Hāla O Naue
- Ke Kali Nei Au (Hawaiian Wedding Song)
- Ke Aliʻi Hula Mamo
- Lei ʻIlima
- Kāhuli Aku Kāhuli Mai
- Kawohikukapulani
- He Eia
- Puamaeole
- Kimo Hula
- Nōhili
- Pānī Au

In his more than 50 years of performing, Mahi Beamer has become a legend in Hawaiian music, performing in venues all over Hawai'i and the Mainland, singing and dancing *hula* and perpetuating Hawaiian arts and culture.

Hawaii's Mahi Beamer is significant both as the full-length debut of Mahi's lithe, pure falsetto and the first recording of the compositions of his grandmother, revered Beamer matriarch Helen Desha Beamer.

Helen learned music notation from Queen Lili'uokalani and was one of the first graduates of the Kamehameha School for Girls, in 1900. She gained a reputation as a talented composer and singer, becoming the choir director for Haili Church in Hilo.

One thing she didn't become was a recording star. Not only was recording technology rare in those days, Helen never intended her compositions for a public audience. Many of her songs were gifts to friends and family members. "Kawohikukapulani," for example, one of Helen's most well known compositions, was written for her youngest daughter, Helen Elizabeth, during her wedding preparations.

So while Helen's songs were treasured by those who knew them, the majority were never committed to tape, and in fact existed only as handwritten notes on various papers when she passed away in 1952. Her daughter Harriet worked diligently to collect and transcribe them all, but it would fall to Mahi Beamer to bring them to life again.

After all, Mahi had learned to play and sing at his grandmother's knee. Gaye Beamer said, "Grandma saw in him the natural talent. He had his own muse that he was blessed with at birth, and she recognized that. So when all the other children were out playing, he was practicing the piano."

When Mahi attended Kamehameha Schools, his music teacher also saw his talent and recommended he pursue a formal music education at the University of California at Santa Barbara.

Mahi did this, majoring in piano for two years. He put school on hold, though, and got a quick initiation into public performance when his sister Nona enlisted his help for a family tour she was planning, one that would travel down into Mexico and then

Edwin Mahiai Copp Beamer: A legend in Hawaiian music, after a half-century of performing and perpetuating culture and the arts.

continue across the United States, sharing *hula* and Hawaiian songs with audiences along the way.

"When we met Nona in San Francisco, she said, 'We have an audition tomorrow, and you're playing guitar.' I was like, 'I don't play guitar!' She said, 'You're playing the guitar.' So I stayed up all night and learned chords on the guitar. I practiced all the songs, and the next day we did the show. Incredible the things that happen out of necessity."

The Beamer family tour enjoyed a great deal of success, and the group ended its journey with a concert at Little Carnegie in New York City. Mahi resumed his formal education at Juilliard, where he did well, although he claimed to have been a lazy student. "My ear could hear everything from a very early age, I knew the melodies and so I would harmonize them automatically," he said. "My teacher would say, 'Now you know that's not what's written.'"

He paid the bills by performing in the legendary Hawaiian Room of the Lexington Hotel, where so many Hawai'i stars have played over the years. In 1951, the military draft for the Korean War brought Mahi back to Hawai'i, where he served for two years at Schofield Barracks. Fittingly, he was assigned to the 264th United States Army Band, and became "the most outstanding glockenspiel player in all of Hawai'i," as Mahi recalled with a smile.

His reputation was growing, and while still in the army, he began performing at nightspots around Waikīkī. By 1954, Mahi had

Out of necessity, Mahi taught himself to play guitar the night before an important San Francisco audition.

top billing at the Queen's Surf, and by 1957, he was getting attention from major record labels. Decca released a single of Mahi performing "Kawohikukapulani," but it was Capitol Records that signed him to record two albums in 1959.

Mahi recorded his debut in the Punahou School auditorium with Don McDiarmid, Jr., who was at that time Capitol Records' representative in Hawai'i. Mahi's aunt Harriet and his sister Sunbeam sang along with him.

McDiarmid recalled that Mahi was very nervous, because it was his first full album: "Fortunately, I had provided a gallon of screwdrivers backstage, so it bolstered his confidence. We did the first two songs, and I kept pushing him. I didn't give him time to think about it."

In fact, they managed to record two albums that day. "It was so incredible, because everything was done with one take," said Mahi. "Except for when an ambulance went by with its siren, and we had to stop. Another time, birds flew into the auditorium and were making a racket. Otherwise we just went."

Those first two albums, *The Remarkable Voice of Hawaii's Mahi Beamer in Authentic Hawaiian Songs* and *More Authentic Island Songs by Mahi . . . Hawaii's Most Remarkable Voice*, became instant classics, documents as they were of Helen Desha Beamer's legacy.

There was a real hunger for her traditional music, said Mahi. "For the old Hawaiian people, it was so pleasing to their ear, this beautiful music and poetry. The *kupuna* loved it. And the kids who were

going away to college took my album with them. It was a little bit of home for them."

Radio personality Harry B. Soria, Jr., said Mahi Beamer's debut became a must-have for every record collection. "It was very traditional, very clean, very high class Hawaiian, with the traditional implements and *hula*. It was very authentic. He's had a long career since, but that moment captured his incredible voice at its prime."

It also captured Helen Desha Beamer's music, preserving her legacy for future generations and ensuring the continued performance of her songs – in 2000, Kamehameha Schools dedicated its 78th annual Song Contest to her, commemorating her influence on Hawaiian music and her graduation from the school 100 years earlier.

Mahi's sister Sunbeam sang with him at his recording debut in Punahou School's auditorium.

21

KAINOA
Marlene Sai, 1962

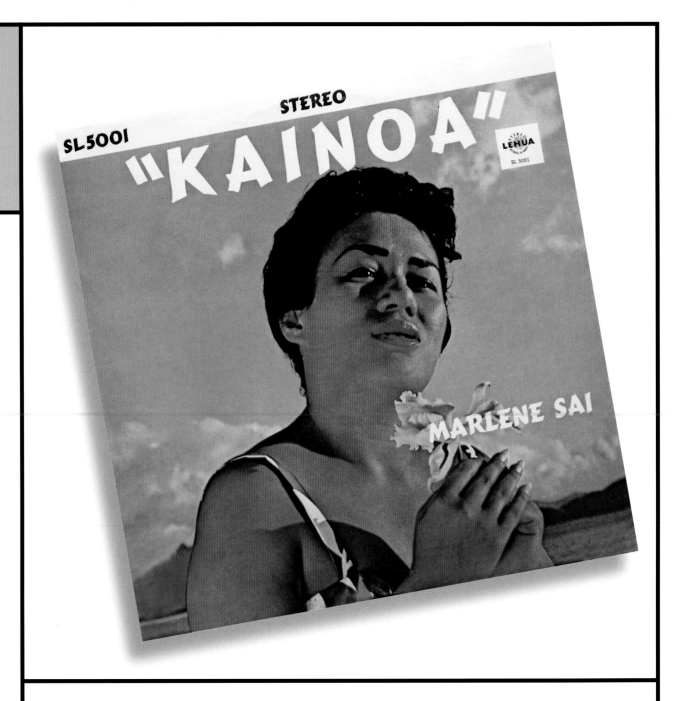

- *Kainoa – J.L. Taka*
- *Kaulana Na Pua –*
  E. Prendergast
- *Haunani Mine –*
  E. Lovey Lui
- *Lovely Kauai – B. Saks*

- *Naka Pueo – S. Kaeo*
- *Paoakalani – Liliuokalani*
- *I'll See You in Hawaii –*
  T. Todaro
- *Crushed Flowers –*
  B. Saks

- *Kuu Hoa – P. Beamer*
- *Ke Ahi Wela –*
  J. Kaholokula
- *A Million Moons –*
  A. Iona
- *Te Reva Nei I Au*

When Marlene Sai was in the 10th grade at Kamehameha, her uncle Andy Cummings taught her a song that would stay with her for the rest of her life. In fact, "Kainoa" would make her a star.

Cummings, one of Hawai'i's finest composers and musicians, happened to be living with the Sai family in Kaimukī at the time. When Sai returned home from school one day, she found her Uncle Andy plucking away on his '*ukulele* on the front steps.

"Before I could start my homework, Uncle Andy would make me sit on the steps to learn this pretty song, 'Kainoa,'" Sai recalled. "It was written by a friend of his, Jimmy Taka, who was dying of cancer. Jimmy wrote it for his wife, Margaret Kainoa Taka. Uncle Andy helped Jimmy put the song to meter and put it down on paper, and I grew to love the song."

The instrumentation of "Kainoa" was simple, unadorned, and easy for any skilled musician to pick up. Its lyrics, though modest, came from the heart.

> *I'm waiting on a warm and sunny seashore*
> *Yearning for the one that I adore*
> *My love is true*
> *I'm thinking of you*
> *Forever I will love you, Kainoa*

The song became the mainstay of Sai's repertoire. When friends or family asked her to sing at school or at a backyard lū'au, she would sing "Kainoa." Naturally, Sai chose this song when, at age 19, she got the chance to perform for Don Ho at his mother's club in Kāne'ohe, Honey's.

"After I graduated from Kamehameha, I started working weekends at a travel agency in Waikīkī," Sai said. "After we were pau work this one Sunday, we decided to drive to Honey's, because one of our friends knew Donald, who managed the place. We played music in the car on the way over, someone had a guitar, and I was singing. When we got to Honey's, my friend told Donald, 'This wahine can sing, you know,' and Donald called me up."

Sai hummed a few bars of "Kainoa" for the club's guitarist, who effortlessly picked up the tune. The guitarist happened to be the young Sonny Chillingworth, now one of Hawai'i's *kī ho'alu* (slack-key guitar) legends. With Honey's musicians behind her, Sai filled the small venue with her sweet contralto.

Her performance blew the audience away. Before Sai left the club, Ho told her he wanted to book her for a real show. She left her phone number with him. But when one week passed, then two, with still no call from Ho, Sai thought, "*Ugh that guy*, and I never bothered with it," she laughed.

Until one weekend, when Sai was driving

home on Kalākaua Avenue in Waikīkī. In her rearview mirror, she spotted a white and green Ford Thunderbird weaving in and out of the cars behind her. The erratic driver pulled up alongside her and jumped out of his car. He was shirtless, his dark hair wind-blown. Sai rushed to roll up her window.

"This guy comes up to my window and said, 'Eh, you remember me from Kāne'ohe? The guy with the organ?'" Sai remembered, laughing. "I'm wondering, *Who are you?* But he kept talking, talking, and then oh, *that* guy! I rolled my window down, and he said, 'I lost your number, but I want you to come down to Honey's tonight to sing.'"

Sai agreed, eager to make a few extra dollars. Several local record executives turned up at Honey's that night, hoping to sign Chillingworth. Legendary producers Herbert Ono, George Chun and Bill Murata were in

the crowd, an intimidating audience for Sai's club premiere.

"Sonny, who was always so kind, said to me, 'You sing for them,' and I said, 'No, they're here to listen to you,'" Sai recalled. "He said, 'Don't worry. I can always record. These guys should hear you.'"

As she had done just weeks earlier, Sai performed "Kainoa." The producers were overwhelmed by the mature, full-bodied voice of the stunning, 19-year-old woman before them. Chun and Ono convinced Sai to join the fledgling label Sounds of Hawai'i.

Sai agreed. Her first-ever recording, however, wasn't made under the most ideal circumstances. Sounds of Hawai'i hadn't even finished building its new studio. Nevertheless, Chun, the producer, wanted to record Sai immediately. He improvised, setting up a studio inside Honolulu Rapid Transit's bus terminal on Alapa'i Street.

"We recorded in the still of the night,

Above: At the International Marketplace, Marlene joins Duke Kahanamoku at the launch party for the **Sunday Camera Show** *and* **Hawaii's Happiest Luau.** *Right: With the host at a Waikīkī taping of the* **Mike Douglas Show.**

when things were settled and quiet," Sai said.

At first, they recorded only a 45 rpm single, which included "Kainoa" and "Kaulana Na Pua." Sai was one of the first artists to record "Kaulana Na Pua," translated as "Famous Are the Flowers." The classic song, written by Ellen Wright Prendergast, decries the 1893 overthrow of the Hawaiian monarchy.

"Kainoa," of course, became an instant hit on local radio stations, catapulting the young Sai to starlet status. It wasn't long before Sai headed back into the studio to record an entire album.

"I had all the musicians from Honey's behind me – Sonny Chillingworth on slack-key guitar, Tony Bee on 'ukulele, Gary Aiko on drums, Benny Saks on xylophone and Don on the organ," Sai said. "We had a ball."

Crowds packed into Honey's for Sai's weekly gigs, curious to see the woman behind the song.

"Marlene came along right when Hawaiian music was changing," said veteran radio personality Honolulu Skylark. "The way it was recorded, the styling of the recording itself, really set new ground. At the time, we had very few female vocalists, and this was a contemporary, fresh voice from a very young, beautiful woman. She presented a style of singing that was different from that of a *kupuna* aunty singing Hawaiian changalang."

It didn't take long for legendary promoter Kimo McVay to catch on. He sought out Sai, convincing her to leave Honey's to perform at his Waikīkī supper club, Duke

Kahanamoku's at the International Marketplace.

Ho didn't want to lose his star performer, but he accompanied Sai to Duke's, anyway, to make sure she "was taken care of." Of course, Duke's later became the launching pad for Ho's own career.

"I was really oblivious, because I didn't know what entertainment life was all about," said Sai, who went on to record more than 20 albums, including several in Japan. "I come from a family where we always had music around us, and I thought everyone sang. I just thought this was the way it was. It took me a long time to realize what an exceptional gift I had, and I am grateful."

Marlene Sai has appeared many times in the persona of Hawai'i's Queen Lili'uokalani.

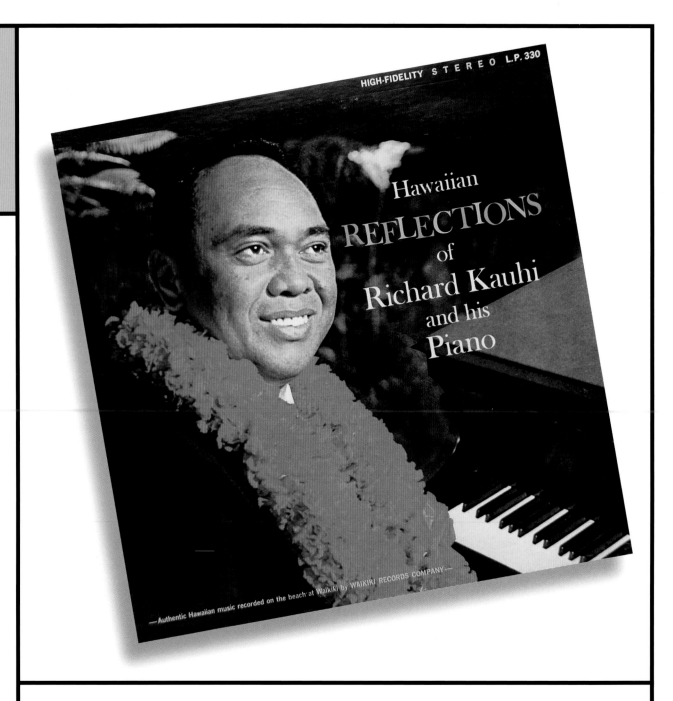

- *Kaahumanu*
- *Marcella Vahine*
- *Pua Maeole*
- *Kona Kai Opua*
- *Pua Carnation*

- *He Ono La*
- *Muliwai*
- *Minoi Minoi –*
  (La Sweet)
- *Lei Lokelani*

- *Kamakani Kaili Aloha*
- *E Mau*
- *No Ne*
- *On a Coconut Island*
- *Leahi*

Many consider Richard Kauhi to be the godfather of modern Hawaiian music. He was one of the first to incorporate jazz elements into local music, playing with the Kalima Brothers and with his own quartet in the '40s. *Reflections* shows Kauhi a decade later in a softer mood, showing the influence of his Palm Springs lounge gigs. The production strips everything away to focus on Kauhi's piano and his dusky voice, to memorable effect.

Kauhi started making a name for himself at an early age. He won first place in KGMB Radio's "Territorial Amateur Hour Contest" with his piano-playing skills when he was just 10, and began playing with the rowdy Kalima Brothers at the tender age of 13. Part of his precocity was born of necessity. When Richard was 11, his mother died of diabetes, and his father contracted tuberculosis and was confined to Leahi Hospital. Richard took to wandering the streets and staying with whoever would let him spend the night.

One of his regular hangouts was the Kapahulu Theater, and it was here that Jesse Kalima came upon Richard in 1942. The Kalima Brothers were at that time one of the most popular bands in Honolulu, but their piano player, Henry Mucha, had been drafted into the war effort, so Jesse was looking for a replacement.

Older, more traditional musicians sometimes criticized the Richard Kauhi Quartette (including, from left, Jimmy Kaku, Richard Kauhi, and Johnny Costello) for "jazzing up" Hawaiian music.

Kauhi had a growing reputation as a pianist, and Jesse persuaded him without much trouble to join the band. What else did he have to do, after all?

The young teen was soon playing with the Kalimas in clubs all over town, as well as recording hit songs with Bell Records. The

A collection of songs chosen for their emotional significance, Reflections of Richard Kauhi and his Piano *was recorded in just two days.*

collective earned the nickname "1,000 Pounds of Melody," for their literal and figurative heavyweight status.

It was an impressive career for someone so young, but by the age of 19 Kauhi was yearning for his own spotlight. He amicably left the Kalima Brothers and set about assembling his own quartet with Mark "Sonny" Kamaka, Johnny Costello and Jimmy Kaku.

By all accounts, Kauhi was an exacting band leader, demanding nothing but the best from himself and the others. In fact, the quartet rehearsed their piano-driven, four-part harmony sound for almost a year before they played in public.

Kauhi's nephew, local radio personality Brickwood Galuteria, said his mother used to tell him about those first practice sessions: "They used to rehearse and rehearse and fight and rehearse and fight and rehearse. Until it was acceptable to Richard, and then they would go out."

The Richard Kauhi Quartette went into the Bell Records studio in 1948 to lay down their first songs, and the finished product was, as Galuteria succinctly described it, "Too tight, brah. Too. Fricken'. Tight." They became an immediate sensation all over Hawai'i with hits such as "Lei Pakalana" and "Kiss Me Love."

Kauhi's new musical style didn't appeal to everybody. Betty Rapozo Kauhi, whom Richard would marry in 1951, said "He was the very first to incorporate those four-part harmonies into Hawaiian music. But at the time, he was ridiculed by the elder musicians. They put him down because they said he was 'jazzing up' the Hawaiian music."

Kauhi said he was only embellishing a beautiful art form with his piano "tinkling," and in spite of the tut-tutting of the *kupuna*, the Quartette were constantly in demand, playing to packed houses at Felix's Florentine Gardens, The Ginza Nightclub and many other spots around Waikīkī.

Unfortunately, in 1951, quartet member Sonny Kamaka returned home to Maui for health reasons. The quartet lineup cycled for a while, but Kauhi began making solo trips to San Francisco and Los Angeles and was eventually persuaded to move for good by Sam Singer, an agent with the Music Corporation of America. He played in Palm Springs and Hollywood for more than 15 years, developing a softer, more lounge-y sound.

Reflections, released in 1965 by Waikīkī Records, was the second solo album Kauhi cut while on the Mainland; the first, *Hawaiian Sunset*, was, according to his wife, a somewhat undistinguished, "bread and butter" job.

Reflections was also recorded quickly, in just two days, with just Kauhi and his piano, but what set it apart was its personal theme. The album really was an assortment of Kauhi's reflections – each song was chosen for its emotional significance to him or someone he loved. "Lei Lokelani," for example, was especially for his wife; it was their love song. She said that, although she has a "tin ear," Richard taught her to sing it with him, he on the melody, she on the harmony. He couldn't get her on record, though – the album version of the song is a solo performance.

"Pua Carnation" was a quiet gesture of defiance. Betty said Richard recorded it because Bell Records wouldn't let him back in his days with the quartet. "When he was young, he always wanted to record that song, because that was one of his parents' favorite songs," Betty said. "Someone on the board of directors at the record company said he didn't want that song. So this was kind of a 'Ha ha, here I am recording this song now' thing."

So the album went, songs dedicated to old friends, his parents, the Kaʻahumanu Society Girls, a radio jockey named Blind Joe whom Kauhi had loved listening to as a kid. Although he never recorded another album before his death in 1979, *Reflections* stands as a distillation of everything that made Kauhi great – a swinging, inimitable piano-playing style, and the heart to back the music up.

His wife Betty mused, "He was just a musicians' musician. He loved what he did with a passion. He loved life and he loved people. When people came through his life, he never forgot them."

Richard Kauhi: A swinging piano-playing style, and the heart to back it up.

23

THE BEST OF THE BROTHERS CAZIMERO, VOL. 1
The Brothers Cazimero, 1987

- Home in the Islands
- Pupu A'o Ewa
- Ka Wailele O Nuuanu
- The Beauty of Maunakea
- Haleakala
- Rainbow Connection
- Hawaiian Spirits Live Again
- Nani Hanalei
- E Kuu Lei
- Tropical Baby
- These Hidden Valleys
- Pua Hone
- Island in Your Eyes
- Ka'ena
- Waika
- Come Become

The Brothers Cazimero have become one of the most successful groups in the history of Hawai'i music. In the 1970s, they started a recording career that would span several decades and produce more than 30 albums.

Although they made a name for themselves playing with The Sunday Manoa, one of the earliest groups of the Hawaiian Renaissance, Robert and Roland had played together professionally long before that. As children, they performed with their family's band.

"Mom and Dad rehearsed on Thursday nights, and we all started out by listening in the bedroom, watching, listening and singing, eventually learning the words," Roland said. "Robert started arranging my sister, Robert and [me] into a three-part harmony. We were maybe 6 or 8."

Robert added: "Because of our parents' involvement in the music, every child was brought into it. There were instruments in the house and a lot of singing. We really thought that every family in the world was doing it. We were so immersed in music."

The Cazimero family toured military clubs on O'ahu – their father played guitar or steel; their mother, the drums. Fans familiar with Robert's skill on bass and Roland's genius on 12-string guitar might be surprised that neither started out playing those instruments. Robert's first instrument was the piano, and it was actually Roland who first learned to play bass – a small child at the time, he had stand on a stool to reach the neck of the instrument.

Their lifetime of playing together is evident on *The Best of the Brothers Cazimero, Vol. I.* Although the album compiles favorites from only the first decade of their work as a duo – "Home in the Islands," "Nani Hanalei" and "Rainbow Connection" – fans should have guessed there was much more to come.

Roland (left) and Robert Cazimero: "We really thought that every family in the world was doing it. We were so immersed in music."

"At the beginning, there wasn't much to do as far as a mission; it's a job," Robert said. "Today, it's the whole idea of longevity and immortality. Long after our physical bodies are gone, the music will live on. We try real hard today to make sure that if this is going to be forever – that's what albums are, forever – it should be worth it."

24

GABBY PAHINUI WITH THE SONS OF HAWAII

Gabby Pahinui and the Sons of Hawaii, 1962

- Na Ono Na La Na Kupuna
- Pua Alani
- Waialae & Holona
- Pua Mohala

- Panini Pua Kea
- Nani Kaua'i
- Hale Aniani & Lani Ha'aha'a
- Hilo E

- Ulili E
- Haleakalā
- Hanalei Bay
- Lei No Kai'ulani

Newspaper columnist Sammy Amalu once wrote that the Sons of Hawaii sang "of life as it really is – hard, a little sad, a little whimsical, sometimes a little bawdy, but always good merely to be living." People could relate to songs such as "Panini Puakea," and no one could sing them like the Sons – slack-key legend Gabby Pahinui, 'ukulele virtuoso Eddie Kamae, bassist Joe Marshall and steel guitarist David "Feet" Rogers.

Although the members had played on other albums, this release marked their debut as the Sons of Hawaii. While all four were superb at their craft, their casual, lively performances were aimed toward the common man. The Sons knew how to entertain a crowd. Ask anyone who ever had the good fortune of seeing them play at The Sandbox, once located in Sand Island.

"Every Thursday, Friday and Saturday, the club was filled – there was joy every night," Kamae said. "People would yell, 'We want this song!' While me, Feet and Marshall just flowed, Gabby was such a showman. He would dance the *hula* – I never seen anything like it. And he'd get people to dance with him. He had the magic."

None of the Sons could speak fluent Hawaiian. Pahinui, in particular, sometimes mispronounced Hawaiian words. Hula Records producer Don McDiarmid, Jr., would be the first to hear about it.

"Every time I put out a new album, I'd get a call from the *tutu* (grandma) ladies, and they'd give me heat about his pronunciation," McDiarmid laughed. "Even when I hired people to sit down and teach him and we finally think we got it right, sure as hell, there are two wrong words in there."

That didn't stop people from listening to the Sons. People overlooked their one shortcoming, because this band was just too good to miss.

"They were all great musicians, and they enjoyed their jobs," McDiarmid said. "They had fun doing it. It showed when you listened to their cuts. You gotta have that heart, that feeling if you want to sing Hawaiian music."

Gabby (second from right) shares one of many light moments during a session with the Sons: (left to right) Joe Marshall, David "Feet" Rogers and Eddie Kamae.

25

HAWAII'S "SONG BIRD"
Lena Machado, 1962

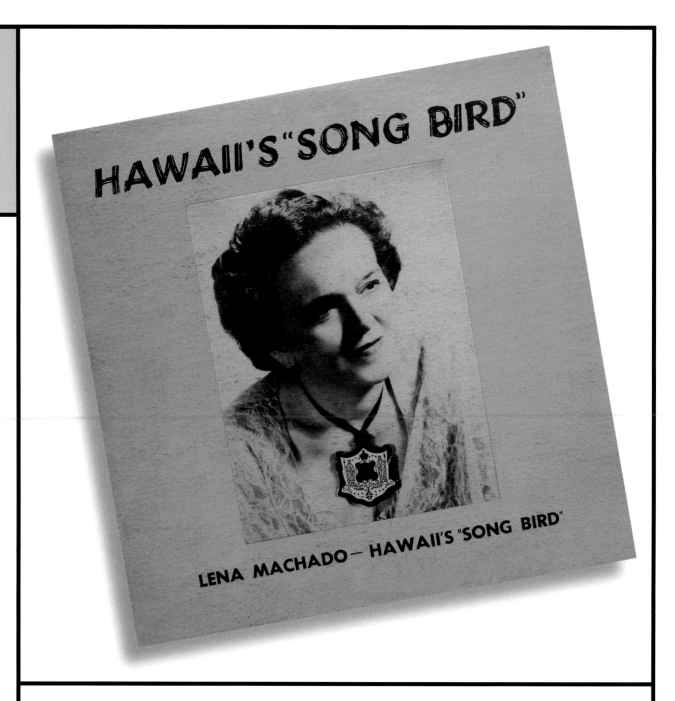

- E Kuu Baby (Hot cha cha)
- Huu Wa Lilii
- Hoonanea
- Holo Waapa
- Mai Lohilohi Mai Oe
- U'i Lani
- Ei Nei
- Moani Ke Ala Ona Pua Makahikina
- Kauoha Mai
- Holau
- Kaulana o Hilo
- Hanakahi
- Mom

Lena Machado was one of the giants in Hawai'i's musical history, not only as a gifted and influential performer, but also as a prolific songwriter, with more than 60 compositions to her credit.

The CD reissue of her landmark 1962 album showcased Machado's recordings from as early as 1927, including an earlier version of "Kauoha Mai (Keyhole Hula)," one of her most famous tunes.

She was known as "Hawaii's Song Bird," a nickname that referred both to her distinctive soprano voice and to the way in which she was originally discovered.

As the story goes, the 18-year-old Machado was singing and picking mangoes high up in a tree on Hotel Street one day in 1922. Marion A. Mulroney, head of KGU, Hawai'i's first radio station, happened to walk by the tree and was transfixed by the beautiful voice that came from above, as if a bird was singing. He immediately signed Machado to a contract with the station, and she was soon a bona fide celebrity throughout Hawai'i.

Machado's career, which lasted almost half a century, brought her to stages all over Hawai'i and the Mainland and established her as one of the most revered icons of Hawaiian music. She sang for the Royal Hawaiian Band, at the San Francisco World Fair, and on television shows such as Harry Owens', revolutionizing the Hawaiian falsetto style along the way.

"Her phrasing and her projection and her presentation was very different from any falsetto singer before her, because everything before her was very slow," commented radio

In the 1930s Lena Machado performed at the South Seas nightclub in Los Angeles, with a backup band that included Benny Kalama and George Piltz on 'ukulele, Sol Hoopii on steel guitar (seated) and Harry Baty (behind Sol) on guitar.

personality and Hawaiian music historian Harry B. Soria, Jr. "She was the first falsetto singer to really learn how to use the microphone, because the microphone was coming up when she was coming up."

Machado's influence can be heard in the works of everyone from Genoa Keawe to Dennis Pavao. Soria said, "She was the one who pretty much set the tone for everything that's been done since then."

26

CANE FIRE!
Peter Moon Band. 1982

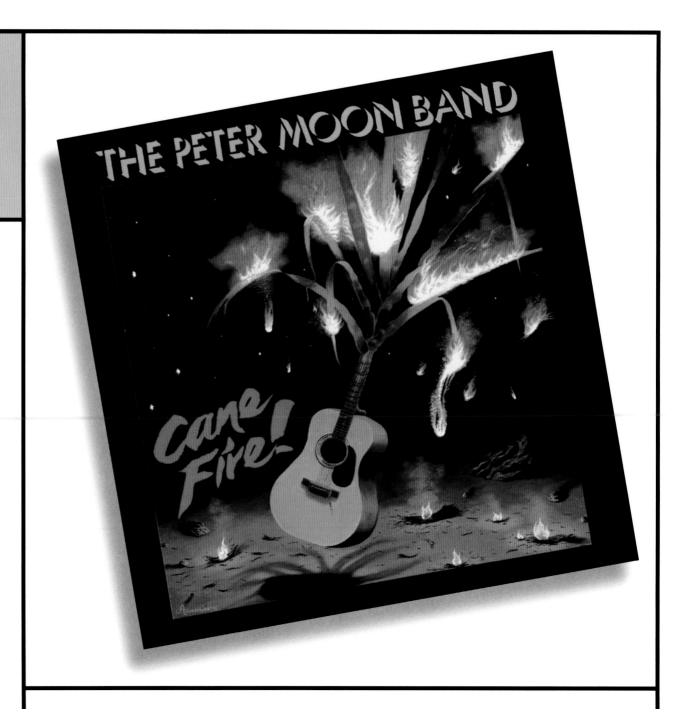

- Ha'aheo E Ka Manu Pīkake
- On a Little Street in Singapore
- Maunaloa
- Pandanus (Instrumental)
- Guava Jelly
- Cheri
- Slack-key Boogie Woogie
- E Pili Mai
- Cane Fire
- Far Too Wide for Me
- Hanohano Hanalei / Ka Ua Loku (Instrumental)
- Hawaiian Soul

When The Sunday Manoa disbanded in 1973, its founder, Peter Moon, took a much-needed break from recording. He shifted his focus to the business side of the local recording industry.

It wasn't until the late '70s that Moon approached producers Steve Siegfried and Witt Shingle at Panini Records, reinvigorated and ready to head back into the studio.

Moon made a musical comeback with his newly formed Peter Moon Band and their first album *Tropical Storm*, which garnered four Nā Hōkū Hanohano Awards in 1979. Three years later, he topped that with his 1982 release of *Cane Fire!* The album earned a total of seven Hōkū Awards, including "Album of the Year," "Group of the Year" and "Song of the Year" for the album's title track.

"I was just trying to make an album with good music," said Moon, a master of the slack-key guitar and ʻukulele. "All of my albums have been an eclectic collection of music, ranging from blues to rock 'n' roll to Hawaiian. I'm influenced by things that go on around me, the music, the musicians, everything."

Like The Sunday Manoa, the Peter Moon Band underwent several shakeups to its roster. The only constant was Moon. *Cane Fire!*, considered one of the group's finest albums, featured an all-star lineup: Cyril and Martin Pahinui, Bobby Hall and Steve Wofford. Guest artists included Merv Ching, William "Smitty" Smith and Ry Cooder.

Each of the group's members was an accomplished musician and a strong vocalist.

Their wide-ranging talents gave Moon the opportunity to make *Cane Fire!* his most diverse album ever. Martin powered through the rock-infused "Cane Fire" and reggae hit "Guava Jelly," the first Hawaiʻi recording of the Bob Marley original.

Cyril's earthy baritone can be heard on the more traditional "E Pili Mai," which earned Moon and Larry Lindsey Kimura a Hōkū as the best original Hawaiian-language composition in 1983. Hall lent his soothing vocals to polished jazz tunes such as "On a Little Street in Singapore," and Wofford graced contemporary pieces such as "Cheri" and "Hawaiian Soul."

"It was nuts, it was crazy," Martin said. "Peter was a great leader and a perfectionist. Sometimes it was hard for us to keep up, because he was going a mile a minute. But we learned so much from him."

Cane Fire! *won seven Hōkū awards for 1982, under the artistic direction of Sunday Manoa alumnus Peter Moon: "I was just trying to make an album with good music."*

27

The Music of George Helm
A True Hawaiian
George Helm, 1977

Recorded in Hawaii

The music of GEORGE
HELM
A TRUE HAWAIIAN

- *Kalamaʻula*
- *Manowaiopuna.*
- *Waikiki*
- *Hoʻonanea*
- *Molokaʻi Waltz*
- *Maile Swing*
- *Kuʻu Pua I Paoakalani*

- *Kamalani O Keaukaha*
- *Pua Mamane*
- *Na Moku ʻEha*
- *Royal Hawaiian Hotel*
- *Kuʻu Lei Aloha*
- *Kimo Henderson Hula*
- *Hawaiian Cowboy*

- *Kalena Kai*
- *Kauoha Mai –*
  The Keyhole Hula
- *Haole Hula*
- *ʻAlika*
- *Moku Kia Kahi*
- *Hiʻilawe*

- *Papalina Lahilahi*
- *Kilakila ʻO Haleakala*
- *ʻAuhea ʻOe*
- *He Aloha No ʻO*
  Honolulu

Perhaps better known as a political activist than as a musician during his lifetime, George Helm became a recording star posthumously with this simple live album.

Originally from Moloka'i, Helm learned to play and to sing falsetto at St. Louis High School in the late '60s, under the tutelage of Kahauanu Lake, who was very impressed by the young man. "I sensed in him something very unusual," Lake said. "Anything he did, his whole heart was in it. All I had to do was refine him. By god, he came along like that."

After a short career at Hawaiian Airlines, Helm became a full-time musician, playing at regular gigs around Honolulu. He also immersed himself in the Hawaiian activism movement, becoming a leader of the Protect Kaho'olawe 'Ohana.

In 1976, between trips to Kaho'olawe to protest the bombing, Helm was playing evenings at the Gold Coin Restaurant in Honolulu. Richard Wong, the restaurant owner, taped some of the performances, but didn't do anything with the recordings until Helm was lost at sea on one of his Kaho'olawe journeys in March 1977.

Wong quickly pulled Helm's electric bass player Steve Mai'i into the studio to fill in the bass lines underneath Helm's trebly guitar work and released the album that May, selling 25,000 copies almost overnight.

Unfortunately, no contract between Helm and Wong had ever been signed, and Helm's family saw no royalties from the album's sales. Radio host Harry B. Soria, Jr., said, "It was like a bootleg. It was an afterthought, but it was brilliant, and Hawai'i was just struck with the guy. But not a penny went to the family."

Producer Michael Cord, who later reissued the album on compact disc, helped to rectify the situation by buying the copyright from Wong and agreeing to pay the Helm family royalties on all subsequent sales.

George's powerful voice and message continue to resonate today. The object of Helm's political crusade was at last realized as well – the Navy finally completed its handover of Kaho'olawe in April 2004, after a 10-year, $460 million cleanup.

Moloka'i native George Helm (at a 1973 Waikīkī Shell fundraiser for the activist group Kokua Hawai'i): His voice – and his message – continue to resonate today.

28

HAWAIIAN STYLE
The Kahauanu Lake Trio, 1964

- *Hu'ehu'e*
- *Pua 'Ahihi*
- *Nani Wale A Ka Mahina*
- *Ku'u Hoa Hololio*

- *Aloha 'Ia 'O Wai'anae*
- *Ka Paniolo Nui O Moloka'i*
- *Wahine Hololio*
- *Punalu'u*

- *Ka Pua U'i*
- *Mālolo*
- *Kaulana Kaua'i*
- *Keolaokalani (Penei No)*

When the Kahauanu Lake Trio released *Hawaiian Style*, one of their earliest albums, in 1964, they sounded more like veteran musicians than young men just breaking into Hawai'i's music scene. To many listeners, Kahauanu Lake, his brother Tommy Lake, and Al Machida exemplified perfection with their contemporary arrangements and musical phrasing of traditional Hawaiian songs. They set the standard for many groups that followed.

"They were such a great influence in our lives," enthused musician Robert Cazimero. "They added a sophisticated kind of elegance that brought along with it the *hula*, and the marriage of both was so sublime. As a singer listening to it, you wanted to mimic it, embrace it. You wanted to do it."

The trio started after Kahauanu returned from serving in the U.S. Army in Korea.

Both Tommy and Al worked for Hawaiian Electric Co. The trio got their first gig playing at the Halekūlani Hotel, the model of old Hawaiian charm in Waikīkī.

"Their act, the Halekūlani Girls, ended up moving to another hotel," Kahauanu recalled. "The general manager at the Halekūlani asked me, 'Wanna take their place?' I said, 'No. We want to make our own place.'"

The Kahauanu Lake Trio offered a musical alternative to the casual backyard sound popular at the time. They were well rehearsed, more refined, rooted in both traditional Hawaiian music and Mainland jazz and swing.

Kahauanu is considered one of the finest *'ukulele* players in Hawaiian music history, in part due to his unique playing style. Although

The Kahauanu Lake Trio (left to right: Kahauanu Lake, Al Machida and Tommy Lake) performs with dancer Mapuana Schneider.

he is right-handed, he plays his ʻukulele, still tuned for a right-hander, left-handed and upside down, confidently strumming, rather than picking, the strings. That's because Kahauanu learned how to play by watching his mother rehearse, mimicking her mirror-fashion.

"His chords are almost impossible for a right-hander to play; that's why his sound is so brilliant," Tommy said. "The tuning of the high string makes it vibrate longer. He hits the low string last, so the intonation is perfect."

Kahauanu arranged compositions where the ʻukulele defined the melody, rather than the rhythm, of the song. In essence, Kahauanu proved that the ʻukulele could play a much more prominent role than it had previously, elevating it from background to lead instrument.

Tommy on bass provided a solid backbone for the trio's arrangements. Al supplied the necessarily fill between Kahauanu's and Tommy's instrumentation.

The brothers, both able to sing falsetto, baritone and tenor, utilized their range to combine with Al's vocals and create rich harmonies befitting the Hawaiian-language classics on the *Hawaiian Style* album.

"Kahauanu has that rare and beautiful diction of the Hawaiian language," said Don McDiarmid, Jr., who produced all the band's albums, including *Hawaiian Style*, over a 30-year period. "He's one of the very few musicians I've produced and had a *tutu* (grandmother) lady call me and say, 'Whatta pleasure it is to listen to them sing in the Hawaiian language.'"

Of course, accurate pronunciation was never negotiable for Kahauanu. As children, he and Tommy learned the importance of speaking the Hawaiian language correctly. Their parents, both fluent in Hawaiian, counted such cultural experts as Vicky Iʻi and Maddy Lam among their closest friends. Mary Kawena Pukui, Hawaiian scholar and co-author of the *Hawaiian Dictionary*, served as their language teacher. Kahauanu consulted with Pukui on the trio's albums, even co-writing several songs with her.

"We concentrated on our phrasing, and a lot of the young singers today don't do that," Kahauanu explained. "You need to respect the language. It's important, because without the resident culture, the music, the language, that is the end of Hawaiʻi."

The trio was as diligent rehearsing songs as they were pronouncing their lyrics correctly.

"If we had to do an album, we played the songs at least eight months, two to three times a week before we made any recording," Kahauanu said. "When we did the first recording, 'Pua 'Āhihi,' we went in there prepared, nailed the intro, the arrangement, the ending. The soundman said, 'You want to hear this?' We were shocked, it was pretty good. He said, 'Pretty good? It's the best!'"

Hawaiian Style includes both upbeat and balladic pieces, such as the classic "Pua 'Āhihi," written by Pukui and Lam, and the traditional "Wahine Hololio," a contemporary medley of two songs in honor of Queen Emma.

Whatever the tempo, listeners can expect that the trio's songs will always complement the *hula*. Kahauanu consistently arranged songs in a way that would promote this ancient Hawaiian art. Of course, he was also married to Maiki Aiu Lake, one of the most revered *kumu hula* in Hawai'i.

"K is a very strict master," said McDiarmid. "He has always known exactly what he wanted, how we wanted it, but he's been right every time. They were perfectly prepared at all times, instruments all tuned, perfectly rehearsed. He's given Hawaiian music the class it really needed to get out of the garage and to the public."

The Kahauanu Lake Trio's career spanned four decades. The trio headlined in some of Hawai'i's top venues, including the Halekūlani, the Kahala Hilton and the Royal Hawaiian. At every performance, the trio made sure to look just as elegant as they sounded, wearing white or dark trousers, long-sleeved collared shirts and fresh flower *lei*.

"They always played acoustic, no amplifier," McDiarmid remembered. "Their playing at the Halekūlani was one of the highpoints of Hawaiian music. Anyone who saw them play under the stars would never forget it."

Hula Records, the McDiarmid family business, produced all of the band's albums over a 30-year period. The four generations of musical McDiarmids: Don, Sr., (below) and (left to right) Don, Jr., Flip and Mac.

29

WE ARE THE CHILDREN
Country Comfort, 1974

- Sun Lite, Moon Lite
- Railway Station
- Make it with You
- Waimanalo Blues

- To Be Lonely
- We Are the Children
- Honky Tonk Wines
- Rainy Day Song

- Country Palace
- Manha de Carnaval

Tom Moffatt once joked that Country Comfort got him out of the group management business.

The group did have a reputation for partying, but they gained an even bigger reputation for their music with this country- and rock-influenced debut. Jimmy Freudenberg, Billy Kaui, Chuck Lee, Randy Lorenzo and Eugene Matsumura, Waimānalo boys all, honed their sound every weekend at The Sty in the Niu Valley Shopping Center, and they soon landed a recording deal from Trim Records based on word of mouth.

When *We Are the Children* was released in 1974, the soulful English-language ballads took local radio by storm and anticipated the folk rock/Hawaiian hybrids that would become so popular later in the decade.

One of the album's biggest singles, "Waimanalo Blues," was originally written by Hawaiian activist and composer Liko Martin as "Nānākuli Blues." Country Comfort localized the song as a political protest about the development taking place all around them: "Spun right around and found that I'd lost / the things that I couldn't lose / the beaches they sell to build their hotels / my fathers and I once knew." Other highlights included "Sun Lite, Moon Lite" and the Latin-tinged "Manha de Carnaval."

Unfortunately, Country Comfort's mellow sound belied their hard-partying ways, and the band spun out of control soon after the release of their second album. Former member Lorenzo said, "They were doing a bunch of heavy stuff. I had to quit – people

were nodding off onstage. I thought, *This is not going anywhere at all.*" By the end of the decade, both Kaui and Lee were dead of drug-related causes.

Country Comfort were a tragically short-lived band, but they burned brightly while together. This album, with its high production values and radio-friendly songwriting, has remained a touchstone of local music, cited as an influence by such bands as Na Leo, Kalapana, Olomana and the Beamers.

Country Comfort's mellow sound belied the group's hard-partying lifestyle.

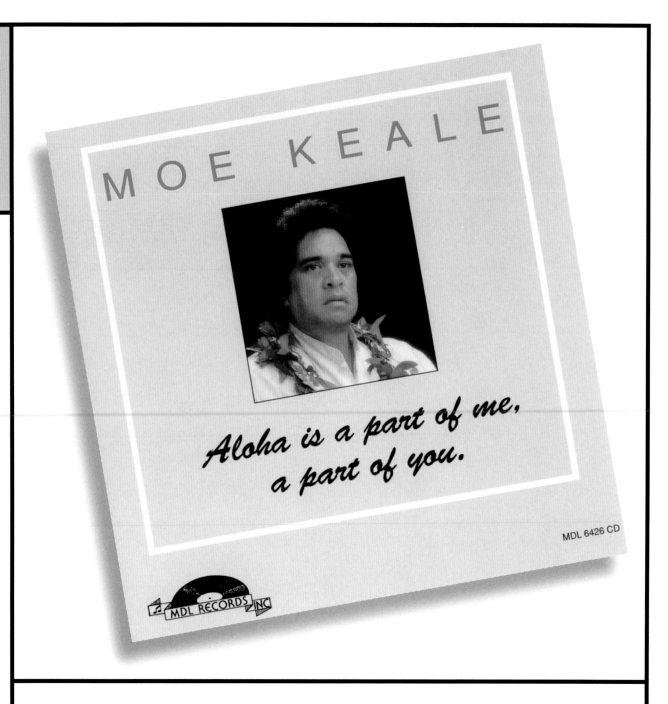

30

ALOHA IS A PART OF ME, A PART OF YOU
Moe Keale, 1986

MOE KEALE

Aloha is a part of me, a part of you.

MDL 6426 CD

MDL RECORDS INC

- *Kaula Ili*
- *Ka Ua Maʻemaʻe*
- *Ki Hoʻalu*
- *Waialae*

- *Mapuna Ka Hala O Kailua*
- *A part of me, a part of you (The Hospital Song)*
- *Aloha Is*

- *Kapalaiʻula*
- *Hanohano Wailea*
- *Na Kama O Hauʻula*
- *Aloha Chant*

Moe Keale was already a well-known entertainer in the Islands by the time he released *Aloha is a part of me, a part of you*. In the previous 26 years, Keale had performed with several groups, including the iconic Sons of Hawaii, and appeared on more than a dozen television shows. People around the world recognized him as "Truck Kealoha," his character on the long-running *Hawaii Five-O* series.

Aloha, however, signaled the start of a new career for Keale, one in which the spotlight shone squarely on him. This album bumped Keale up from skilled sidekick to superstar.

"That was such a celebration in the Hawaiian community," recalled friend and longtime radio host Harry B. Soria, Jr. "Everybody knew him, everybody loved him, so much *aloha*. He had such a long history, but when he came out with the album, it was just finally, the essence of Moe Keale truly was presented in recording."

Keale was full Hawaiian, something increasingly rare in modern times. His father was a *kahuna* who grew up on the private island of Niʻihau. Keale started playing the ʻukulele at age 6. It was Sons of Hawaii founder Eddie Kamae who helped him understand that the ʻukulele could play leads in songs, not just accompaniments.

Keale also possessed a distinctive voice – a subtle vibrato, pure and affecting, matched only by the voice of his nephew, the late Israel Kamakawiwoʻole.

The album's title derived from two songs: "A part of me, a part of you (The Hospital Song)," written by Danny Lopes, an employee at The Queen's Medical Center, and "Aloha Is," composed by Keale's mentor, Hawaiian cultural resource Pilahi Paki. "Aloha is" sweetly captured Keale's own approach to life. He was as famous in the Islands for his huge heart as he was for his musical accomplishments. Keale passed away in 2002.

The album earned 11 Nā Hōkū Hanohano Award nominations in 1987, including "Song of the Year" for each of the title tracks. Although "A Part of Me, A Part of You" seemed more popular at the time, it was "Aloha Is" that garnered Keale's only award that year.

"In the car on the way home, Moe said, 'I'm kind of disappointed I only won one,'" recalled Keale's widow, Carol. "I said, 'You won the most important one, the one our teacher wrote.' He said, 'You're right. That's the only one that mattered.'"

After his affiliation with the iconic Sons of Hawaii, Moe Keale fronted his own trio before recording the solo album "Aloha is…"
Left to right: David Kaʻio, Moe and Kalani Kupau.

31

HAWAIIAN TRADITION
Amy Hānaiali'i Gilliom 1997

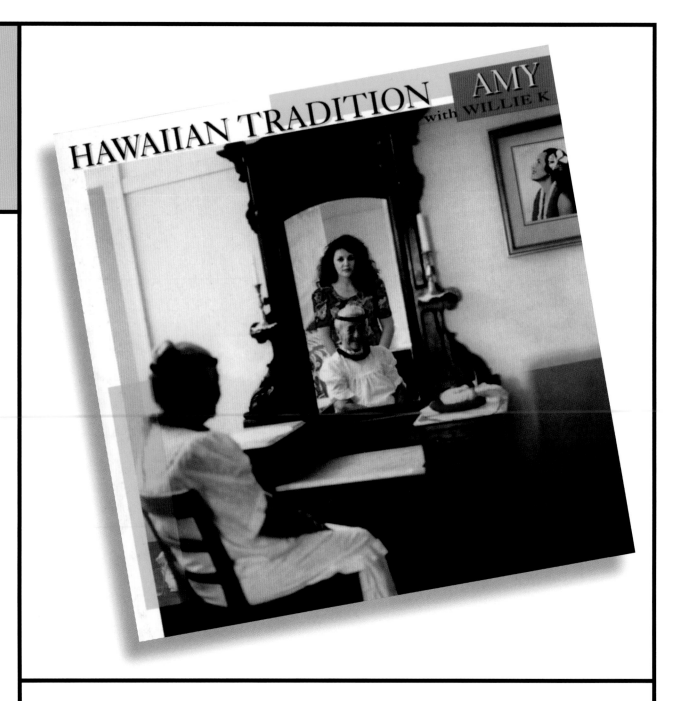

- Hale'iwa Hula
- I Ka 'Āina Kaulana
- Pōhai Kealoha
- Hale Ali'i O Waimaka
- Ho'i I Ka Pūnana
- I Ali'i Nō 'Oe
- Nā Manu O Kalani Nui
- Ua Noho Wau I Nēia Wahi Kaulana
- Lehua'ula
- Pili Mai Nō I Ka Ihu
- Hānaiali'i Nui Lā Ea
- Kaulana Waialua A'o Moloka'i
- Kihawahine

Amy Hānaialiʻi Gilliom puts her classically trained voice to beautiful use on this, her first completely Hawaiian-language album, and the contrast between her traditional *haʻi* falsetto singing and the simple, contemporary backing arrangements of Willie Kahaialii makes for a captivating experience.

The album kicks off with a symbolic passing of the baton from the *kupuna* to the younger generation. Gilliom sings "Haleʻiwa Hula," a composition by her grandmother, Jennie Napua Hānaialiʻi Wood. At the end of the song, Wood herself exclaims, "Maikaʻi kēlā! Himeni hou, himeni hou!" *That's great; sing it again!*

Gilliom originally started out singing jazz and show tunes; after earning a bachelor of fine arts in musical theater from the United States International University in San Diego, she became the house singer at the Ritz-Carlton, Kapalua, on Maui. It was her grandmother who persuaded her to take up the traditional Hawaiian style of falsetto singing. "She definitely set me down the path," recalled Gilliom. "She took me to go see Auntie Genoa, and I sat with Auntie Genoa for a while and learned from her. And I basically learned from listening to all the old albums too. I learned all the inflections and everything."

The next piece fell into place when Gilliom saw Willie K performing "Haleʻiwa Hula" at La Pastaria in Kīhei. "I told him, 'Do you know you're playing my grandmother's song?' He was like, 'Who's this *haole* chick talking to me?' I asked, 'Can I sit in with you?' So I sang in *haʻi*, and he looked at

me like he couldn't believe what was coming out of my mouth."

It was the beginning of their professional collaboration, not to mention a romance that inspired much of this album.

"Most of the songs on *Hawaiian Tradition* are experiences that Willie and I had, places that we've been and literally just written right there," said Gilliom.

32

HAPA

Hapa, 1992

- *Haleakalā Kū Hanohano*
- *Kaopuiki Aloha*
- *Ka Uluwehi O Ke Kai*
- *Anjuli*
- *Lei Pīkake*
- *Olinda Road*
- *Ku'u Lei, Ku'u Ipo*
- *Justin's Lullabye*
- *Ku'u Lei Awapuhi*
- *Oh My Love*

Judging from the composition credits on Hapa's self-titled debut, it's tough to believe that founding member Barry Flanagan had moved to Maui from the Mainland just 10 years before the album's release. In addition to arranging all 10 of the tracks, he composed seven of them, three of which are in Hawaiian.

"When I started getting exposed to more Hawaiian music, I did nothing at all but play music, study and read translations to get a flow of how to compose," remembered Flanagan. "In my life, I've put together poetry and stories. Here, I learned how to put poetry together in the Hawaiian mindset."

Flanagan made sure to consult Hawaiian cultural experts, such as translator S.H. Kīʻope Raymond. Flanagan would hand over his half-English, half-Hawaiian compositions. Raymond would diligently translate them into his native language.

Keliʻi Kanealiʻi, the duo's lead vocalist and 12-string guitarist, grew up in Papakōlea, in Honolulu, more than 6,000 miles away from Flanagan's New Jersey birthplace. Before Kanealiʻi met Flanagan at a 1983 Christmas party, he played in a disco band with Martin Pahinui, the son of slack-key legend Gabby Pahinui.

"Barry was playing Hawaiian music, and I was more into the contemporary James Taylor, Kenny Loggins stuff, even though I'd played Hawaiian music growing up," Kanealiʻi said. "It was a balance in music. We started playing at the party, and it just went from there."

Hapa was eight years in the making. "We played at clubs in Lahaina for about 10 years," Kanealiʻi explained. "Whenever we had money, we'd go into George Benson's studio, record a song, come back out, then go back in when we had enough money."

It was worth it. When *Hapa* hit radio stations, Hawaiʻi couldn't get enough of songs like "Kuʻu Lei, Kuʻu Ipo" and "Lei Pīkake." Flanagan's skilled songwriting and slack-key stylings, combined with Kanealiʻi's haunting vocals and musical dexterity, reminded listeners of the musical creativity that abounded during the Hawaiian Renaissance of the 1970s. The album garnered six Nā Hōkū Hanohano Awards in 1994, including "Album of the Year" and "Group of the Year."

Although Kanealiʻi left Hapa in 2001 and Flanagan turned Hapa into a five-piece ensemble that includes vocalist Nathan Aweau, this 1993 debut remains one of Hawaiʻi's top-selling albums.

Papakōlea native Keliʻi Kanealiʻi and Mainland transplant Barry Flanagan joined forces to produce one of the top-selling Hawaiian albums of all time.

33

VANISHING TREASURES
Hawaiian Style Band, 1992

- *Let's Talk Story*
- *No Ke Ano Ahiahi*
- *Living In A Sovereign Land*
- *Deeper In Love*
- *Love And Honesty*
- *Live A Little*
- *Vanishing Treasure*
- *What's Going On*
- *Kaimana Hila*
- *Dance*

The Hawaiian Style Band was a success story in reverse. The group had a hit radio single before they recorded an album, won a Hōkū award before they assembled a band, and released a hugely successful album before they ever played a live concert.

It all started with a little jingle Wade Cambern and Bryan Kessler penned for surf shop Local Motion. The two had been playing around Honolulu together for years as Jetstream, occasionally writing promotional tunes for local businesses.

Rob Burns, the founder of Local Motion, tapped them to compose some original music for a series of television commercials. The first piece Cambern and Kessler came up with was "E Nana," a breezy, reggae-tinged piece that sounded less like a commercial than a made-for-the-beach radio single.

"People were calling in to radio stations and wanting to hear the Local Motion commercial song," Cambern remembered. "That was the first indication that we had something marketable."

Of course, "E Nana" wasn't an actual song – it existed only in 30- and 60-second versions – but its creators didn't make that mistake again. The next Local Motion jingle, "Live a Little," was released as a full-length single. It was an instant hit, and won a 1991 Hōkū award for "Best Single."

"On the evening of the Hōkūs, we just decided then and there to start working on a full-length CD," Cambern said. The original concept was to form a band with a revolving, all-star cast of members – the focus was to be the music rather than specific personalities. For instance, the cover of *Vanishing Treasures* features a colorful block print in lieu of the usual band photo.

In 1993 Vanishing Treasures earned a Hōkū for the Hawaiian Style Band (clockwise from lower left: Robi Kahakalau, Wade Cambern, Merri Lake McGarry and Bryan Kessler).

The duo began writing songs for the album, but Kessler said they quickly realized they needed some help. "We wanted to add more vocals, but more importantly," he admitted, "we wanted to write some Hawaiian stuff, and Wade and I had no clue about how to do that. So we started looking for someone to help us translate our lyrics into Hawaiian." This is when Robi Kahakalau, who was at the time singing with Ernie Cruz and Troy Fernandez at Moose McGillicuddy's, entered the picture.

She knew Hawaiian and had a beautiful voice as well, one that Cambern compared to that of Stevie Nicks. The one thing she didn't have was studio experience.

On the first day of recording, Kahakalau froze up trying to sing "Love and Honesty." As she recalled: "I wanted to sing it exactly right, but instead of singing with feeling, I was calculating how they wanted me to

The success of Vanishing Treasures *was followed by promotional appearances on radio and television.*

sing. I saw them whispering to each other behind the thick glass, and I was like, *Oh my god! Here's my career, gone.*" She got over her initial jitters quickly, though, and nailed the song the next day.

Merri Lake McGarry also joined the group, and Rob Burns used his local surf connections to bring in an all-star cast of guest appearances – Israel Kamakawiwoʻole, the Kaʻau Crater Boys, Cyril and Bla Pahinui, Del Beazley.

Cambern said, "I think some people were skeptical of a couple of *haole* boys trying to put a Hawaiian CD together, but

Rob kind of smoothed the whole deal over and got all these guys to come to the studio."

The combination of strong songwriting and talented musicians made for productive recording sessions. "It just became this time of creativity and camaraderie and music," Kessler said.

When the album was released, it jumped to the top of the local music charts and became inescapable on the radio. "Every time you turned the dial, there would be another Hawaiian Style Band song," he said.

But even with the heavy airplay and brisk sales, even after *Vanishing Treasures* won the 1993 "Contemporary Album of the Year" Hōkū award, the public was a bit confused by the semi-anonymous nature of the band. Was Bruddah Iz part of the band? The Pahinuis?

Kahakalau said, "People never used to recognize me, because there were no pictures on the CD, but after the Hōkūs, they started to recognize my face. They would go, 'Eh, you that singer, yeah, Hawaiian Style Band?' That was my name for the longest time: not Robi, but 'the singer from Hawaiian Style Band.'"

Even the band members weren't sure how to translate the album, which was very much a studio creation, into a live experience. Kessler said, "We got to this point where people were requesting us, throwing gigs our way. Good gigs. Except we didn't know how to do it, because we couldn't get all these artists together that had originally performed on the album."

They ended up assembling a backing band from among their musician friends and dividing the singing duties among Cambern, Kessler and Kahakalau.

The Hawaiian Style Band made its live debut at that year's Waiki'i Music Festival on the Big Island, and the audience response finally drove home to the band members what an impact they had on Hawai'i.

Cambern said, "I'll never forget. We were there for several hours prior to going on. It was a lot of fun, lot of groups going up. But when we got on stage, everybody just rushed forward to the stage, and there was just a surge of energy happening."

The Hawaiian Style Band's next album, *Rhythm of the Ocean*, also did very well, but tensions were beginning to develop within the group, and Kahakalau decided to take advantage of the band's revolving clause to pursue a solo career.

The third album didn't have the same feel as the first two, nor their popularity, and the band split after its 1995 release. Their songs remained radio staples, however, and the band remained alive in the public's imagination – years later, each of the former members was still getting asked regularly when the next Hawaiian Style Band album was coming out.

Singer Robi Kahakalau left the band to pursue a solo career after the release of a second album, Rhythm of the Ocean.

34

HONEYMOON IN HAWAII
Hilo Hawaiians, 1960

- *Haole Hula*
- *Hole Waimea*
- *He Aloha No O Honolulu*
- *Hawaii Calls*

- *Enchanted Isles*
- *Nani Waialeale*
- *Ke Kali Nei Au (Wedding Song)*
- *He Punahele*

- *E huli No'i Mai*
- *Medley : Waipio, Makalapua, Kuuipo*
- *Uilani*
- *Pua Ona Ona*

The Hilo Hawaiians, made up of Bunny and Kihei Brown, Edward "Mona" and Puni Kalima, and Arthur Kaua, was one the most notable groups to come out of the historic Haili Choir in Hilo. They sang beautiful vocal harmonies, led by Kihei's falsetto.

The Choir, which was formally established in 1902, influenced not only the Hilo Hawaiians' singing, but also their sense of musical history.

According to the album's liner notes, "One selection, 'He Aloha No O Honolulu,' arranged by Kihei Brown, is done in three parts: the first is sung in the five-note scale, which was the only scale the Hawaiians had prior to the arrival of the missionaries; the second shows the missionary influence and brings a bit of New England to Hawaiian music; thirdly, as the song is heard today." It was a clever bit of reinterpretation that presaged the coming Hawaiian Renaissance.

In 1956, USO sponsored the Hilo Hawaiians to tour throughout Europe, from Switzerland to Scotland, performing Hawaiian music and *hula* for audiences who had never heard or seen anything like it.

Band leader Bunny Brown said the response was always enthusiastic. He especially remembered a show they performed during a stopover in New York City for the Hiroshima Maidens, a group of Japanese women who had traveled to the city to receive plastic surgery for the scars they suffered during the atomic blast in Hiroshima.

"The funny part was that they weren't supposed to be smiling or laughing or anything, but you could see they started to smile," Brown said. "They seemed to have enjoyed it."

Honeymoon in Hawaii was the Hilo Hawaiians' debut album, recorded while on tour in Chicago. The album became very popular and was released in several editions, the most notable one with a deluxe, 58-page, full color booklet that is now a collectible. Sections in the booklet included a brief Hawaiian history and such essays as "Malihinis and how they got here" and "What should you bring to Hawaii?"

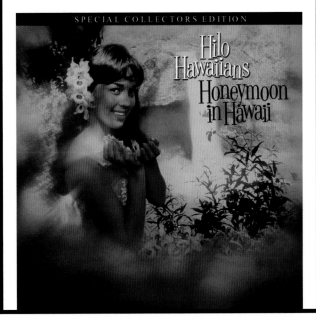

In each concert on their extensive worldwide tours, the Hilo Hawaiians made it a point to include folk songs of host countries in their repertoire. Left to right: Bunny Brown, Kihei Brown, Arthur Kaua, Mona Kalima and Puni "Buddy" Kalima.

Honeymoon in Hawaii *sported a new cover upon re-issue.*

35

HAWAIIAN COUNTRY
Melveen Leed, 1975

- Kamakani Kaili Aloha
- The Music of Hawaii
- The Hawaiian Wedding Song
- Haole Hula
- Paniolo Country
- Honolulu Blue and Green
- Walk through Paradise & Jesu Me Ke Kanaka Waiwai
- Hiilawe
- Baby Pakalana
- Hano Hano Molokai
- The Green, Green Grass of Home
- My Little Grass Shack
- Me Oe E Au E Hele Pu (Closer Walk with Thee)

Melveen Leed is one of Hawai'i's most eclectic performers. With her rich, bluesy vocals, she has taken on everything from jazz to katchi katchi to Latin and pop music. But it was her one-of-a-kind fusion of Hawaiian and country music that endeared Leed to fans of both these genres, two types of music that originated thousands of miles apart but complemented each other nonetheless.

Although Leed is known for her impeccable fashion sense, she has always considered herself a country girl. She grew up on Moloka'i, where "everybody used to know everybody," as she explained, before moving to O'ahu in her senior year in high school. She's also a former beauty queen – she earned fourth place in the 1962 Miss Hawai'i competition – but insists that wasn't any of her doing.

"My grandmother did that to me!" Leed laughed. "It wasn't me, because I was so tomboy. I wanted to beat up all the other contestants. Real tita, you know."

Leed credits her sense of style to her mother, who always reminded her to accessorize and check her outfit in a full-length mirror before leaving the house. But she inherited much more from her mother and father – their vocal talents.

"Nobody was singing professionally, but we all enjoyed music," Leed said. "It's common in Hawai'i, the whole family singing in the garage, you know. I've been singing since I was three years old."

Like those of several other local entertainers, Leed's career started spontaneously at a nightclub in Waikīkī. Entertainers performed Hawaiian standards, songs that locals already knew by heart. It wasn't uncommon for performers to call audience members to the stage to sing a number or two.

When Leed was 19, entertainer Sterling Mossman summoned her to the stage at the Queen's Surf supper club.

"My friend said, 'Let's go sing,' and I said, 'I don't want to,'" Leed recalled. "She said, 'I'll bet you $5.' That was a lot of money in those days, so I said OK. I told the waitress, 'Give me a napkin and a pen.' Then I wrote on the napkin, 'Please call Melveen Leed up. She's very good.'"

Though Leed admitted they weren't the cleverest sentences she'd ever thought up, they worked. Leed easily won over Mossman, as well as the audience, with her soulful sound and local-girl charm. Whenever Leed visited his show, Mossman always called the young songstress to the stage for a few numbers.

It wasn't until 1966, however, that Leed received her first real break in Waikīkī's music scene. At age 21, she started singing with the

Melveen's grandmother joins her at the 1962 Miss Moloka'i Pageant.

Berne' Hal-Mann Dance Band at the Hilton Hawaiian Village Garden Bar. "People came to dance when I sang," said Leed, who later joked, "Now if they try to dance while I sing, I say 'Sit down. It's my show.'"

Leed's stint with the dance band coincided with the glory days of Waikīkī, when locals crowded clubs to see such entertainers as Don Ho, Al Harrington and Marlene Sai.

"In the old days, Waikīkī was jumping, and we supported one another," said Leed. "We went across the street to see each other perform after our own gigs. Nowadays, you don't have that camaraderie – it's gone, completely gone," she added, with characteristic frankness. "You can quote me on that. Musicians today need to learn from us, the teachers, the pavers."

Of course, in the 1970s, Leed became more associated with Nashville, Tennessee – clear across the country – than Waikīkī. It started with Charles G. "Bud" Dant, the bandleader and composer who convinced Leed to give country music a try.

He even introduced her to Owen Bradley, a pioneer of the "Nashville Sound," which attracted a broad audience with its combination of pop, rock and country music. Bradley produced country greats such as Patsy Cline, Loretta Lynn and Conway Twitty.

"Bud was responsible for me having anything to do with country music," Leed said. "He sent Owen one of my tracks. When Owen heard it, he sent for me. It was the first time I'd been to Nashville."

Nashville was the recognized center of country music production, known as "Music City." On her first visit, Leed sang at the Grand Ole Opry. She was one of the first Hawaiians to perform at the country music landmark.

"It was decorated with flowers, and it just smelled and looked like Hawai'i," Leed said. "I handed out flowers to women in the audience. It was wonderful, because I was representing Hawai'i."

Leed recorded *Hawaiian Country* in both Nashville and Honolulu. Dant arranged the album's 13 songs – in both English and Hawaiian – with clear-cut Nashville-style instrumentations. "Paniolo Country" and "Walk Through Paradise" became the album's biggest hits, establishing Leed's reputation as "Hawai'i's Country Girl." She has since recorded six albums in Nashville.

"I was just thrilled to death to sing with these musicians, who've sung with people like Patsy Cline, but they were so humble, simple folk, how I am," Leed said. "They reminded me so much of Hawai'i."

Melveen broke new ground with her Nashville-style interpretations of Hawaiian songs, becoming one of the first Hawaiians to perform at the Grand Ole Opry.

36

POI DOG

Rap Reiplinger, 1978

- *Portuguese Huddle*
- *The Young Kanakas*
- *Room Service*
- *Haikus*

- *Mahalo Airlines*
- *Fate Yanagi*
- *Lolo Telethon*
- *Date-a-Tita*

- *Local Argument #7*
- *Loving You Is Surfing You*
- *Japanese Roll Call*

Poi Dog is the only non-music album on this list (well, unless you consider "Fate Yanagi"), but it couldn't possibly be left out. It's commonly agreed that no other Hawai'i comedy album has given such keen insights into local culture, been so imitated and just plain been so *funny.*

Rap Reiplinger made a name for himself in the early '70s, performing at the Territorial Tavern as part of the comedy group Booga Booga, with James Grant Benton and Ed Kaahea. But it was this solo debut that cemented his reputation as a comedic genius. Even his own later work would never match this album.

Reiplinger's comedy was fueled by a brilliant intellect. He was instantaneous with a comeback and was constantly coming up with new material.

Leah Bernstein, president of Mountain Apple Co., said that when *Poi Dog* producer Jon de Mello gave Rap a typewriter to type out his material, "He was just coming up with all this new stuff, and he literally burned out the typewriter. I had to take it in to Kaimuki Typewriter to get it fixed, and the store manager asked me, 'Did your kid pound on this or something?' I had to tell him it was Rap Reiplinger."

In the studio, Rap had better success at transferring his ideas to the record. "He was ahead of his time," said musician Jake Shimabukuro. "He used multi-tracking techniques just how we do with our instruments, creating conversations, creating dialogue between himself and himself, or three or four different people talking to each other. He was just amazing at creating atmosphere."

Nor has time been unkind to *Poi Dog*, as it is to so much comedy. Rap's material sounds not at all dated; it's as funny now as it was in the '70s. Mr. Frogtree's room service frustration, Auntie Nelly Kulolo's Date-A-Tita service – they all just seem to get better and better.

In **Poi Dog**, *his solo debut,* *Booga Booga alumnus Rap* *Reiplinger introduced a* *cast of now-legendary* *local characters.*

37

RABBIT ISLAND MUSIC FESTIVAL
Gabby Pahinui, 1973

- Waialae
- Ho'oheno Keia No Beauty
- He Nohea 'Oe I Ku'u Maka

- Makee Ailana
- Haleiwa Hula
- Ka Loke O Maui
- Ua Nani Kaua'i
- Pua Lililehua

- Pua Mamane
- Kaua'i Beauty
- Palolo
- In the Garden of Paradise

Rabbit Island Music Festival captures the legendary Gabby "Pops" Pahinui at his backyard best. Here, the slack-key icon jams with four of his sons – Martin, Cyril, Bla and Philip – and old friends, including music greats Sonny Chillingworth, Leland "Atta" Isaacs, Manuel "Joe Gang" Kupahu and Randy Lorenzo.

It was a concept album. Rabbit Island is a bird sanctuary off the coast of East Oʻahu, near Pahinui's Waimānalo home. No music festival takes place there, but with lively tracks such as "Hoʻoheno Keia No Beauty" and "Palolo," Pahinui and his pals didn't need one. The recording sounds as casual and lively as the backyard jam sessions the Pahinui home was known for.

"We recorded this album a year after he did his first album with his sons, *Gabby*," said Steve Siegfried, who co-produced *Rabbit Island* with Witt Shingle and Lawrence Brown of Panini Records. "This time, we wanted to have it more loose, more of a party atmosphere."

Siegfried hired boats to take Pahinui and the musicians out to Rabbit Island, where photographer David Cornwell shot pictures for the album. As soon as Pahinui stepped off the boat, he fell facedown in the water, Siegfried recalled. Pahinui laughed it off – that was his style. One album photo shows a shirtless Pahinui, happily standing on the shore, waving his arms just like the terns behind were flapping their wings.

"It was great fun recording these guys," Siegfried laughed. "Sonny, who we were in awe of because he's such a great singer and slack-key player, was an old friend of Gabby's. When Gabby asked Sonny to be on the album, the guy almost started crying. Sonny said, 'Pops, anything you want, I'll be there.'"

Combining Pahinui with other veterans such as Chillingworth and Kupahu (on bass) and younger, rock 'n' roll-influenced musicians like his sons and Lorenzo (on electric guitar) made for 12 dynamic tracks.

"Gabby was so open to new music and willing to give people a chance," Siegfried said. "It was great fun recording with those guys. They knew how to party."

Gabby Pahinui makes like a seabird on the shoreline of Mānana (Rabbit) Island, framed by the cliffs of Makapuʻu. The photo shoot for the album was arranged with special permission of the State Department of Land & Natural Resources.

38

JACK de MELLO
PRESENTS
THE BEST OF
Emma

A Collection of 25 HAWAIIAN CLASSICS
Orchestra and Chorus Directed by Jack de Mello

- *The Hawaiian Wedding Song (Ke Kalie Nei Au)*
- *Kamehameha Waltz*
- *Waikiki*
- *I'll Weave a Lei of Stars for You*
- *Here in this Enchanted Place*

- *The Wonderful World of Aloha*
- *Tutu*
- *Ku'u Pua I Paoakalani*
- *Song of the Sea*
- *'Akahi Ho'i*
- *Song for Ka'iulani*
- *Nani Wale Lihu'e*

- *Ku'u Ipo I Ka He'e Pu'e One*
- *Ka Wai 'Apo Lani*
- *Wai'alae*
- *Pride of Waiehu*
- *The Queen's Prayer*
- *Ma Lana'i Anu Ka Makani*
- *Moloka'i Nui A Hina*

- *Liliko'i*
- *Song of Happiness (Kokoni Sachiari)*
- *Song of the Flower Drum (Chinese Folk Song)*
- *Chamarita (Portuguese Folk Song)*
- *Arirang (Korean Folk Song)*
- *I'll Remember You*

Each of the 25 classic songs on this album reminds listeners why Emma Veary is considered one of Hawai'i's most glorious voice artists. No modern-day singer comes close to her skill in performing monarchy era songs, including Veary's signature piece "Kamehameha Waltz."

"Emma was classically trained as a singer, but when she sings Hawaiian songs, she sings them with this incomparable Hawaiian soul and passion," said Byron Yasui, professor of composition and music theory at the University of Hawai'i.

Although Veary is not the oldest living person on this list, it's possible that she has enjoyed the longest music career. It started with a call from her kindergarten teacher, who informed Veary's mother, Hannah, of her 5-year-old daughter's spectacular voice.

Her parents decided to let Veary perform at local venues, including Hawaiian Town, The Tropics and the Niumalu Hotel, now the site of the Hilton Hawaiian Village. Veary also performed at various movie theaters in Honolulu – including Hawai'i Theatre, the Princess Theatre and King Theatre – that featured stage shows between films.

"When I was 6 or 7, I sang at the old Wai'alae Country Club on the weekends, and I met all the big stars who came through, like Bette Davis and Rochelle Hudson," Veary recalled. "The place had a roof that, if you pressed a button, would open up and you could see the stars above. I just loved it. The workers would be setting up, and they'd say, 'OK, Emma, you can go open the roof now,' and I'd run to push the button."

Veary thrilled spectators with her surpris-

ingly mature interpretations of Hawaiian classics, songs of a bygone era. Though just a child, she pronounced every Hawaiian word correctly. It wasn't socially acceptable to speak Hawaiian at the time, so Veary never learned the language. Her mother, however, was a respected Hawaiian cultural expert who made sure her daughter's phrasing was flawless.

Island radio host Harry B. Soria teasingly called Veary "The Kid." "She had been on one

of his radio shows on KGU in the late '30s, *Waikīkī Beach Broadcast*," said Soria's son, Harry B. Soria, Jr., also a longtime local deejay. "She was only 8 years old, and she was already a trooper – so much experience, so much class and elegance, she made Hawaiians feel good about their music and culture."

Music wasn't just Veary's career. It filled her home in Kapahulu. Her parents, brother and sister sang and played music. Other budding musicians lived in her neighborhood,

Even as a young performer, Emma Veary "made Hawaiians feel good about their music and culture."

including Richard Kauhi, Johnny Costello and Jimmy Kaku.

"We lived there during the war years in the early '40s when we used to have blackouts, and serenading was the greatest gift of all for us," Veary reminisced. "People aren't aware now that in the old days, people would take their sleeping bags and sleep on your lawn, never worry about anything. Guys picked up their 'ukulele or guitar and started singing – what a special time we lived in."

theater production *The Flower Drum Song*.

"Both times, I chose to stay with my family," Veary said. "Lord knows where I'd be today, if I hadn't. I'd set my sights on having a singing career, but I didn't want to be separated from my family."

Years later, Veary eventually would leave Hawai'i. After studying under vocal instructor Richard Vine at the University of Hawai'i, she worked on several off-Broadway productions – including *Showboat* and *West Side*

Tracks on **The Best of Emma** *were compiled from four solo albums that Emma recorded with Jack de Mello (conducting at upper left).*

Veary passed up two chances that could have catapulted her to Shirley Temple-like success. Her first opportunity came in 1941, when tinsel-town producer Joe Pasternak asked Veary to come to Hollywood. A second offer came from legendary actor Gene Kelly, who met Veary when she auditioned for the

Story – and at Mainland conventions.

In the 1960s, Veary re-launched her music career in Islands. When she started performing at the Royal Spaghetti House in downtown Honolulu, word spread quickly. Island residents crowded the small restaurant to see the operatic soprano. Even non-

Hawaiians were delighted to hear live classical music in Honolulu. Veary's interpretations of monarchy-era songs set her apart from the pack of *hapa-haole* music entertainers in Waikīkī.

That's why conductor and producer Jack de Mello enlisted Veary to sing on his four-album masterpiece, *Music of Hawai'i*. The series took well-known Hawai'i songs and arranged them for a full symphony orchestra in London. He also recorded four solo albums with Veary, from which *The Best of Emma*'s 25 tracks were compiled.

"It was such a wonderful experience," Veary said. "Jack is so very, very creative, and I have so much respect for that man and what he's done for Hawaiian music."

Of course, Veary's biggest fan was her husband, Hal Lewis, better known in the Islands as No. 1 disk jockey J. "Akuhead" Pupule. Famous for his on-air pranks and controversial programming, Lewis wasn't shy about promoting his wife. He plugged her gigs enthusiastically, and when Veary's first album debuted, he played her songs as often as possible. Lewis affectionately nicknamed her "Old Golden Throat."

Even after she returned to Hawai'i, Veary was still in demand around the globe. She traveled to New York to perform at Radio City Music Hall and, in 1973, to London to sing at the five-star Savoy Hotel.

When The Royal Spaghetti House became too small to accommodate Veary's audience, she moved on to the Halekūlani. She later performed at the Kahala Hilton, the Moana Surfrider and at Kemo'o Farms in Wahiawā with Charles K.L. Davis. In true

classical style, Veary sang with two pianos or one piano and a harpist. At the Monarch Room at the Royal Hawaiian, she was backed by an entire orchestra.

Veary now lives in Pukalani, Maui, but continues to perform occasionally. Since the mid-1990s, she has co-starred in "Merry Christmas with Friends and Nabors," an annual concert at the Hawai'i Theatre with entertainer Jim Nabors.

"I tell people that the vocal cord is a muscle, and unless you exercise it, it's not gonna perform for you," Veary said. "I tell Jim, 'We're going to be walking out in walkers soon doing this show,' because we've been doing it so long. Each year, we say, 'Think we'll do it again next year?' till we get the call. And everybody still asks me to do 'Kamehameha Waltz,' even if it's for a Christmas show."

Emma performed at many of Hawaii's top venues, accompanied in classical style by two pianos or a piano and a harp.

39

TROPICAL HAWAIIAN DAY
Ka'au Crater Boys, 1991

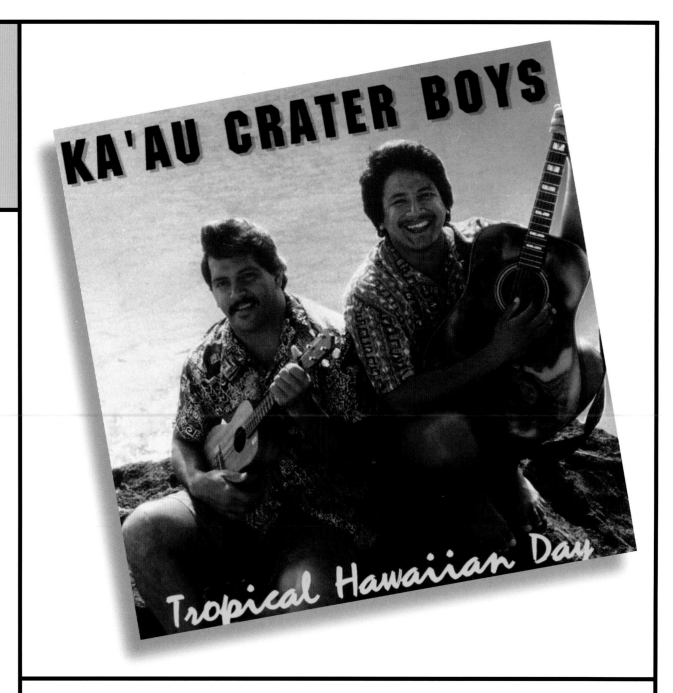

- *Tropical Hawaiian Day*
- *No Ke Ano Ahi Ahi*
- *I Hear Music*
- *Aue Te Nehe Nehe / Maui Girl*
- *Nobody's Darling but Mine*
- *Kawika*
- *Rhythm of the Falling Rain*
- *Hāna Calls*
- *Still the One*
- *Guava Jam*
- *Stand by Me*
- *Sela Moku*
- *Here's a Lei*
- *Sweet Lei Ka Lahua*

Ka'au Crater Boys split up in 1997, but fans still identify Ernie Cruz, Jr., and Troy Fernandez with the group that rocked Hawai'i in the '90s. That's even after both artists released solo albums, with Cruz winning two Nā Hōkū Hanohano Awards for his 2001 release, *Portraits*.

"Almost anywhere I go in Hawai'i, some guys don't even know my name, they just go, 'Eh, Ka'au!'" Cruz said. "It's OK, I know what they mean. I go, 'Eh, brah. Howzit?'"

It's easy to see why folks have a hard time letting go. Ka'au Crater Boys released their first album, *Tropical Hawaiian Day*, in 1991, and locals went crazy for Fernandez's wizardry on 'ukulele and Cruz's caressing vocals and smooth guitar rhythms. The band spun out upbeat originals such as the title track and "Hāna Calls," as well as fresh remakes of such tunes as "Rhythm of the Falling Rain" and "Still the One."

"The way I knew we were kinda big was one day, we did a gig at Princeville on Kaua'i," Cruz said. "I went surfing out at Hanalei, and on the way in, there were some boys playing 'ukulele. I wanted to see what they were playing. It was 'Tropical Hawaiian Day,' and I thought, 'This is cool. The kids are digging us.'"

Many credit Fernandez with rekindling interest in the 'ukulele in the '90s. Even 'ukulele sensation Jake Shimabukuro considers Ka'au Crater Boys one of his greatest influences.

"I must've been in intermediate school the first time I heard 'Tropical Hawaiian Day,' and I thought, *That can't be an 'ukulele!*" Shimabukuro said. "It was just a different sound I wasn't familiar with, kind of backyard jamming but refined and sophisticated at the same time – just ingenious. Ka'au's music inspired a lot of new players to play 'ukulele, like myself."

Cruz and Fernandez recorded four albums together, each one more successful than the one before. Before their last album together, *Making Waves*, even hit stores, customers had pre-ordered thousands of copies.

"We had no formula, we didn't have a plan to take over Hawai'i," Cruz said. "The 10 years just flew by. I'm grateful for that part of my life, which was a good stepping-stone for me to the music I'm playing now."

The Ka'au Crater Boys (Troy Fernandez, left, and Ernie Cruz, Jr.) recorded four albums together before moving on to solo careers.

40

LOYAL
Loyal Garner, 1981

- *Hello Honolulu*
- *Chotto Matte Kudasai*
- *Blessed with Another Day*
- *Home in the Islands*
- *Behold Lai'e (with Robert Cazimero)*
- *I Don't Want To Go Away*
- *Pua Olena*
- *Koke'e*
- *How Great Thou Art*
- *Blind Man in the Bleachers*

Loyal Garner earned the nickname "Lady of Love" while hosting a telethon for the Muscular Dystrophy Association. It seemed entirely appropriate for a woman whose rich, soulful voice and warm personality had enraptured Hawai'i for more than 20 years.

During the telethon, it looked like the pledges would fall short of that year's goal. Garner pled tearfully with the television audience to call in more pledges. She was successful. The telethon eventually exceeded its fund-raising target.

Garner "always sang from her heart," said music resource Alan Yoshioka of Harry's Music Store. "*Loyal* expresses the warm and tender side of her. One of the songs, 'Blind Man in the Bleachers,' moved us to tears whenever she performed it."

Loyal wasn't Garner's first album, but with memorable hits such as "Chotto Matte Kudasai," this was the recording that made Hawai'i fully appreciate the spectacular performer. Garner was a large woman, with the carriage of an opera diva and the warmth of a caring mother. On stage, those traits were even more obvious.

"There are people who know how to sing, but can't entertain," said Melveen Leed, who was one of Garner's closest friends. "She did both. She talked to the crowd, made them a part of her act. She could make them cry, make them laugh; that's what it's all about."

Garner lived and breathed music. She taught herself to play the piano and the bass. She later studied music at the University of Hawai'i while performing at the Golden Dragon at the Hilton Hawaiian Village. In 1975, she became a popular act on the local music scene with performances at the 'Ilikai Canoe House.

She came by her artistic talent naturally. Garner's mother, Alice Keawekane, was a famous Hawaiian chalangalang singer and dancer. Her sister is a respected *kumu hula* and her brother Kimo is also a musician.

Garner, however, didn't pursue the traditional Hawaiian route. Many of her songs were pop oriented, characteristic of the kind of music popular in the rest of the country.

"When this album came out, her career, her solo act, her visibility all came together at the same time," said longtime radio host Harry B. Soria, Jr. "After years of hard work, everything was happening for her. Finally."

Loyal poses with her close friend Melveen Leed during one of the pair's many joint appearances.

41

Hoʻoluana
Mākaha Sons of Niʻihau, 1991

- *Hualālai*
- *Kumulipo/E Pua Ana Ka Makani*
- *He Inoa No Piʻilani*
- *Ka Manokalanipō*

- *Nohili E*
- *Mehameha/White Sandy Beach*
- *Aliʻi ʻIolani*
- *Pua ʻAla Aumoe*

- *Ka Hanu ʻO Evalina*
- *Take a Walk in the Country*
- *I'll Remember You*

Ho'oluana was the last album recorded by the Mākaha Sons of Ni'ihau before Israel Kamakawiwo'ole's departure, and it shows the band at its creative peak. The group, which also featured Louis "Moon" Kauakahi and John and Jerome Koko, was so busy during the late '80s and early '90s with touring and other projects that the album took four years to record, the group ducking into the studio whenever they could for quick sessions between trips.

"A lot of times we would go in, leave, and then when we came back we didn't know what we recorded last time. We'd have to relearn the song," band leader Kauakahi said.

In the time it took to record *Ho'oluana*, the Mākaha Sons also released a live album, *Mākaha Bash 3*, and Israel released a solo album, but the packed schedule didn't hurt the cohesive feel of the album – Kauakahi's single-minded vision ensured that the music was in the signature Mākaha Sons style.

Producer Kata Maduli and engineer Jim Linkner raised the bar on the production levels, giving the songs a more bass-heavy mix and extracting disciplined performances from each of the players. "I don't think they had ever had anybody cracking the whip over them, but they had this fundamentally great sound," said Linkner, "so we were just being sticklers on the technical side. When the voices came out, wow."

"Mehameha/White Sandy Beach" and "Take a Walk in the Country" epitomize the Sons' easy harmonizing and traditional guitar stylings while introducing string arrangements from the Honolulu Symphony that gave the songs an unprecedented polish.

According to the band members, the recording sessions, though widely spaced, were smooth and productive, and there seemed to be little indication that Israel would be leaving the band. "It caught us all by surprise. We never really knew why, and we probably won't," said Kauakahi.

Israel left on a high note. The album became the Mākaha Sons of Ni'ihau's biggest-selling album to date, and garnered five Hōkū awards, including "Group of the Year" and "Album of the Year."

Ho'oluana *was the group's last album before the departure of Israel Kamakawiwo'ole. Left to right: Jerome Koko, John Koko, Iz and Louis "Moon" Kauakahi.*

42

IĀʻOE E KA LĀ, VOLS. I, II, III & IV
Palani Vaughan, 1973–1980

Volume I:

- *Heʻeia*
- *Kaulana Ia Ka La*
- *Kokohi*
- *Kauliluaikeanu Waltz*

- *Keloi ʻO Likelike*
- *Kaʻa Ahi Kahului*
- *Iaʻoe E Ka La*
- *ʻAkahi Hoʻi*

- *Poni Moʻi*
- *Ninipo*
- *Hawaiʻi Ponoʻi*

With his rich baritone voice and classic good looks, Palani Vaughan seemed destined to be the next Alfred Apaka. But after a stint in Waikīkī performing romantic *hapa-haole* lullabies like "Honolulu," he gave that idea up.

"My heart gravitated toward more traditional Hawaiian music," Vaughan said. "In the '60s and '70s, there was a lot happening with young Hawaiians trying to understand who they were, including me. I was a Hawaiian without roots."

Vaughan found what he was looking for in historic texts about Hawai'i's monarchs, spending years researching Hawaiian culture, language and history. He was among the first of a younger generation intent on learning more about their Hawaiian heritage. The reign of King Kalākaua became Vaughan's focus.

"I realized that, aside from *hula*, people didn't recognize Kalākaua enough for his achievements," Vaughan said. "You could read about his achievements, but you couldn't find them in music. I thought music was a better way of educating the masses."

That led Vaughan to write dozens of songs celebrating Kalākaua's reign, compiling them into the astonishing four-volume series *Iā'oe E Ka Lā*. One of Vaughan's most recognizable compositions, "Ka'a Ahi Kahului," explains how Kalākaua encouraged railroad building in the Islands. Vaughan also resurrected 19th-century songs such as the title track, which was written by a relative of Kalākaua in honor of his historic good-will journey around the globe. Vaughan played an autoharp, which gave these traditional songs a distinctly monarchy era sound, even if they were arranged in a contemporary style.

After the first volume was released, Vaughan began looking the part, growing a thick mustache and mutton-chop sideburns to resemble Kalākaua. His concerts were elaborate, featuring traditional royal costumes and props, such as a replica of the 'Iolani Palace gazebo. Vaughan's work was an integral part of the Hawaiian Renaissance, the cultural reawakening also fueled by other artists such as the Sons of Hawaii and The Sunday Manoa.

"Palani helped perpetuate our Hawaiian culture," said veteran radio personality Honolulu Skylark. "He was so driven in his belief that this history, this language and this art should not die."

Although Vaughan went on to record a second two-volume set of songs honoring Hawai'i's royalty, it "was overshadowed by *Iā'oe E Ka Lā*," he said. Considering what a triumph the earlier body of work is, Vaughan's got nothing to be ashamed of.

A student of the Kalākaua era, Palani Vaughan staged concerts and other elaborate productions that featured traditional royal costumes and props, an effort that became an integral part of the Hawaiian Renaissance.

43

THIRST QUENCHER!
Hoʻokena, 1990

- Oli Pale
- Hoʻokena
- Kamukī Hula
- Kimo Henderson Hula
- Haleʻiwa Pāka
- Kūhiō Bay
- Iā ʻOe E Kaʻehukai
- Pua O Ka Mākāhala
- Iā ʻOe E Ka Lā
- Napoʻona Mahina
- ʻŌiwi Medley
- Alu Like
- E Mau
- Hoʻōla Lāhui Hawaiʻi

For much of the 1980s and '90s, the reggae-influenced music known as Jawaiian dominated radio airwaves in Hawai'i. Many local listeners enjoyed the infectious Caribbean beats. Others worried that Jawaiian would eclipse more traditional Hawaiian music.

But the arrival of Ho'okena – Manu Boyd, Glen Smith, Horace K. Dudoit III, William "Ama" Aarona and Gregson "Bozo" Hanohano – reassured purists that real Hawaiian music still thrived in the Islands. The group's debut album opens with a traditional *oli* (Hawaiian chant) and ends with " 'Ōiwi Medley," a mix of three Hawaiian classics that express pride in being Hawaiian. Between the two tracks, the group's rich vocal harmonies and instrumentation can be heard on songs both old and new, including two original compositions, "Napo'ona Mahina" and "Iā 'Oe E Ka'ehukai."

"The Jawaiian influences were really strong in local music, and that's all you heard on the radio," said Manu Boyd, Ho'okena's composer, vocal arranger and *'ukulele* player. "Our style has a contemporary flair to the arrangements, and it gives a presentation of old songs in a more modern way."

Desire to nurture their unique style was the reason Ho'okena insisted on total control over their first recording. Group members kicked in money to establish their own record company, Ho'omau Inc.

"We didn't even approach anybody else," said Smith, lead vocalist. "We just decided we wanted to do it – all under our wings, do what we want to do, do the music we wanted to. Halfway through the record, we already had offers from companies to buy the rights to the recording. We said, 'We started it under us. We're gonna keep it under us.'"

Ho'okena has self-produced all eight of their albums to date. With the departures of Aarona and Hanohano and the return of bassist Chris Kamaka, an original member of the group, Ho'okena is now a foursome. They celebrated their 18th anniversary in 2004.

"Whether we're practicing in our living rooms or singing at the Waikīkī Shell, it makes us feel good to do it," Boyd said. "When we recorded *Thirst Quencher!*, we had no idea how long we'd be together. But as long as there's music and there's *hula*, we will always have a definite role to play."

Ho'okena, which formed its own record company to produce Thirst Quencher!, today includes, left to right, Chris Kamaka, Glen Smith, Horace Dudoit III and Manu Boyd.

44

FLYING WITH ANGELS
Nā Leo Pilimehana, 1995

- *Here in the Rising Tide*
- *When I Think of You*
- *Loving You*
- *Blue Skies above Me*
- *Flying with Angels*
- *Ka Leo O Ku'u Lehua*
- *Soft Green Seas*
- *Still Yours*
- *How Long*
- *Crushed Flowers*

Flying with Angels is a document of independence, the first album by Nā Leo Pilimehana recorded entirely under their artistic control and released under their own label, NLP Music.

The trio, composed of Lehua Kalima Heine, Nalani Choy and Angela Morales, found fame early, with the hit single "Local Boys." The light-hearted ode to – what else? – local boys earned the Kamehameha High School seniors a 1985 Hōkū "Best Single" award.

The girls had stars in their eyes, but their parents had different plans. Choy said, "We were young, and we promised our parents we'd get real jobs and not be musicians, so we had to fulfill that. So we went to college and worked on our careers." They all stayed in touch, but for the next eight years, music stayed on the back burner – the focus turned to jobs, marriages and children.

Then a producer recognized Choy as a member of Nā Leo during a routine business transaction at the bank she worked at, and encouraged her and the others to jump back into music. The success of their return album, *Friends*, affirmed the public hunger for Nā Leo's gentle brand of vocal harmonizing, but the women weren't sure they wanted to pursue music full time, particularly since their existing record contract was not as lucrative or creatively flexible as they wanted.

Heine said, "We were at a crossroads, deciding if we really wanted to do this again. A good friend, Ken Makuakane, said, 'Hey, if you don't like the whole manager/producer situation, just be your own.' He showed us how to set up a record label and how to get started."

Taking a leap of faith, the three quit their jobs and set about recording *Flying with Angels*, with Makuakane as producer. The

majority of the songs were written by Heine, who said, "It was a progression, because we were taking control of things, playing more of our own music. We weren't just the little high school girls people remembered." Growing up was a good thing – the album was a hit, netting Nā Leo four Hōkū awards.

Flying with Angels *was recorded when the three former high school classmates (left to right: Angela Morales, Lehua Kalima Heine and Nalani Choy) quit their day jobs and took a leap of faith.*

45

PURE HEART
Pure Heart, 1998

- *Bring Me Your Cup*
- *Green Rose Hula*
- *Olinda Road*
- *Crazy without You*
- *Ka'ai*
- *Hey Baby*

- *You Came into My Life*
- *Juss' Press*
- *Moloka'i Sweet Home*
- *Waimānalo Blues*
- *On Fire*
- *Star of Gladness*

- *Jake's Prelude*
- *Europa*
- *One Love*
- *Mr. Sun Cho Lee*

Pure Heart's self-titled debut is the most recently recorded entry of these 50 Greatest Hawai'i Albums. In 1998, local listeners couldn't resist the talent and charm of the trio's fresh-faced members – 'ukulele whiz kid Jake Shimbukuro's extreme picking style, Jon Yamasato's earnest vocals and skill on guitar, and percussionist Lopaka Colon's flair for pounding out rhythms.

Songs such as "Hey Baby" and "You Came into My Life" made *Pure Heart* a smash. The album garnered four Nā Hōkū Hanohano Awards: "Island Contemporary Album of the Year," "Album of the Year," "Most Promising Artists" and, by public vote, "Favorite Entertainer of the Year."

"Our whole approach to the band and to the recording was just to have fun," said Shimabukuro. "We weren't so caught up in trying to sell records or win awards. We really enjoyed the music, and we wanted to capture that."

The public considered the group's rise meteoric. But that wasn't the case, Yamasato explained. Pure Heart played in coffee shops, usually without pay, for four years before recording the album.

"Most people think we came out of nowhere, but we were gigging for so long," Yamasato said. "That first album was really the culmination of the four years we'd played together. We'd established this good bank of songs that we always played, and we picked out the most popular ones for the album."

Pure Heart recorded two more albums before disbanding in 1999. All three performers continue to record today. Colon has made guest appearances on albums by other local artists, such as Don Tiki. Yamasato released his first solo project in 2003 – after recording albums with artist Justin and the group Nā 'Ōiwi – and produced the female duo Keahiwai.

Shimabukuro became the first Hawai'i musician to sign with Epic Records, a division of Sony Music Japan, in 2002. He released his third album on the label in 2004.

"We always discussed with each other projects we wanted to do," Yamasato said. "We all had other aspirations, but when I look back, I remember the good stuff. I have good memories of it."

Pure Heart (clockwise from bottom: Lopaka Colon, Jake Shimabukuro and Jon Yamasato) played for years in coffee shops, often for free, before recording their eponymous album.

46

THE SUNDAY MANOA 3
The Sunday Manoa, 1973

- *Eleu, Mikimiki*
- *Nani Kaala*
- *Iuka O Kokee*
- *Manu Ulaula*
- *Ua Like No A Like*
- *Ka Lama Ae One*
- *Waiomina*
- *Pupuhinuhinu*
- *Kahuli Aku*
- *Hilo Hanakahi*
- *Hilo E*
- *A Hawaiian Lullaby*

Guava Jam, the first collaboration by Peter Moon and Robert and Roland Cazimero, introduced Hawai'i to the musical innovation of The Sunday Manoa. Islanders embraced the modern sound, and the album sparked the renaissance of Hawaiian music in the 1970s. But even after their groundbreaking debut, The Sunday Manoa continued to push the boundaries of contemporary Hawaiian music.

It was a tough act to follow, but the trio tried anyway. First they created *Cracked Seed*, which met with limited success, and then they brought out *The Sunday Manoa 3*, the third and final album by the pioneering trio. On *The Sunday Manoa 3*, the group's music benefited from additional instruments and higher production values, resulting in a richer, more embellished sound. More importantly, the album demonstrated the development of its members as individual artists.

"We were all grown up already," Roland confirmed. "There was a lot more experience. On this album, there was a focus by all three of us, versus Peter just focusing and us filling up musical parts. It was something we did together."

Rather than relying solely on Peter's 'ukulele and guitar, Robert's bass and Roland's guitar, the group incorporated less traditional instruments into the mix – an electric fiddle on "Eleu, Mikimiki," a banjo on "Manu Ulaula" and "Ka Lama Ae One," a dobro on "Ua Like No A Like" and a tiple on "Hilo Hanakahi."

"For me, that was why the album was really something," Robert explained. "We recorded half of it in Honolulu, the other half in Hollywood at Capitol Records. There was a string section, and the melding of those instruments along with our voices gave the album a nostalgic feeling."

The significance of these top-notch string musicians became especially apparent on "A Hawaiian Lullaby," the lush, moving composition co-written by Moon and Hector Venegas that begins, "Where I live, there are rainbows…"

"It was cool to hear these professional studio musicians who weren't Hawaiian really enjoying the music along with us," Roland said. "They took the initiative to suggest, 'Can I do this? Can I do that?' Like the ending of 'A Hawaiian Lullaby,' the conductor Sid Feller arranged it, and when the first chair played it, I started to cry."

Clad in matching aloha wear, The Sunday Manoa (left to right: Roland Cazimero, Peter Moon and Robert Cazimero) plays music in the Big Island cowtown of Waimea. Panini Productions captured this and other performances that day in The Waimea Music Festival, an album released a year after Sunday Manoa 3.

47

KAHAIALII
Willie K, 1990

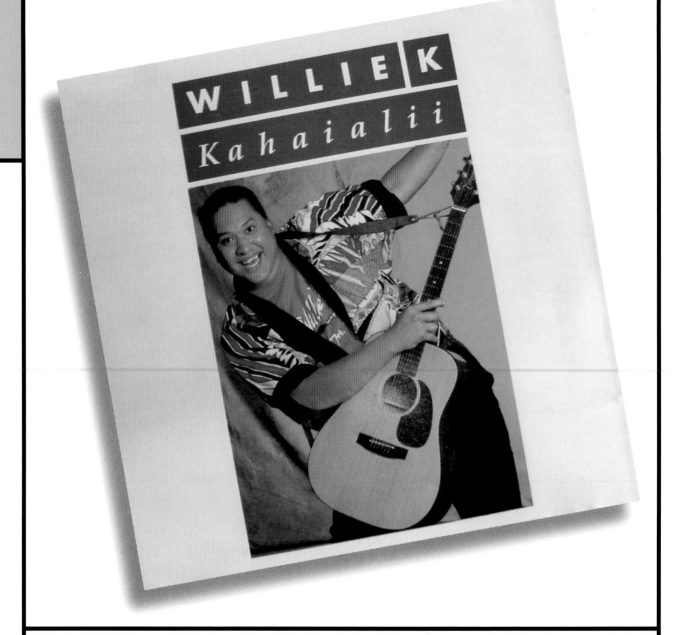

- *Good Morning*
- *Katchi Katchi Music Makawao*
- *You Kuuipo*
- *North Shore Reggae Blues*
- *Spirits in the wind*
- *My Molokai Woman*
- *Hoonanea*
- *Hookipa Surf Song*
- *Tracks of My Tears (Sad Eyes)*
- *Honey Girl*
- *Satisfaction*

Willie Kahaialii is one of the most eclectic performers in Hawai'i (in 2003 he played Eddie in a Maui staging of the *Rocky Horror Music Show*), and this debut album shows his range perfectly. From traditional Hawaiian falsetto on "Hoonanea" to reggae on "Good Morning" to calypso on "Katchi Katchi Music Makawao" to barbershop on "Honey Girl" to electric rock 'n' roll on a cover of the Stones' "Satisfaction" – there's nothing he can't do.

Producer Jim Linkner told the story of a Willie K concert at Aloha Tower Marketplace: "Willy does some Hawaiian music, and then he does a little rock 'n' roll, a Hendrix song. Then he puts the guitar down and starts singing this Italian aria. He's a perfect, natural tenor. Perfect, like Pavarotti. He's got the pipes. He's singing this thing, and it's just building and building. Everyone stood up, and women are crying. He gets done and the audience is just screaming and applauding." A few days later, Willy told Linkner that he had made up the entire aria. Apparently, artist and friend Amy Gilliom had been ribbing him about not knowing classical music, so he bought an armload of CDs and listened to them enough that he could emulate the style.

Kahaialii enjoys confounding expectations – he has said he learned to play Hendrix's song because his father, Kamanu Kahaialii, also a musician, used to pressure him to play only Hawaiian music.

"I'm a completely different type of Hawaiian," said Kahaialii in a 1993 interview for *Honolulu Weekly*. "When [people] hear my album and then they see me on stage, it's two completely different things. They don't see that ... sweet-voiced guy; they see this mean guy that goes up on stage looking like a biker ready to kick anybody's ass ... That's me, I don't want to be stereotyped."

Willie K: a completely different type of Hawaiian.

48

YELLOW BIRD
Arthur Lyman, 1961

- *Havah Nagilah*
- *Yellow Bird*
- *Ravel's Bolero*
- *Autumn Leaves*
- *Arrive Derce Roma*
- *Sweet and Lovely*
- *Bamboo Tamboo*
- *Andalusia*
- *Adventures in Paradise*
- *Granada*
- *September Song*
- *John Henry*

Although Arthur Lyman first tasted fame as Martin Denny's vibraphone player – you can hear his playing on *Exotica* – he later became a star in his own right, playing in a lounge-y, wildlife-punctuated style similar to Denny's.

After the breakthrough success of *Exotica* in 1959, the demand for tiki sounds and instrumental Hawaiiana created a niche big enough for two artists, and Lyman became the Pepsi to Denny's Coke, waging a friendly competition for the ears of America.

"There was enough business to go around; the scene was so big at that time," Harry B. Soria, Jr., remembered. "Vibes were really in, as were jazz influences, so there was a market for Arthur as a solo recording artist."

When Denny left Hawai'i to tour in support of his album, Henry Kaiser hired Lyman as the replacement headliner at the Waikīkī Shell Bar. Hi Fi Records, after seeing the success Liberty Records was enjoying with Denny's records, signed Lyman as their main act. He recorded almost all his albums in Honolulu, and was a fixture at the Shell Bar for the next decade.

Lyman was steadily successful throughout the '60s, appearing on various television shows and touring the Mainland periodically, but his breakout hit was the mellow *Yellow Bird*, which spent 10 weeks on *Billboard's* Top 10 chart in 1961, peaking at No. 4.

He might have been influenced by his former band leader, but Lyman managed to

distinguish himself with his inimitable four-mallet vibraphone playing and his ability to incorporate Hawaiian music into the genre. Singer Nina Kealiiwahamana said, "They both played that exotic sound with the bird calls and the bongos, but you never mistook Martin for Arthur, or vice-versa."

In 1955 (left to right) Arthur Lyman, Martin Denny and John Kramer were the original trio in Don the Beachcomber's Dagger Bar, the tiki-themed lounge in the International Marketplace.

49

ALOHA – CHARLES K.L. DAVIS SINGS AND PLAYS FOR HAWAI'I
Charles K.L. Davis, 1992

- *End of the News*
- *He Ono*
- *Kuu Pua Paoakalani*
- *Akahi Hoi*
- *Koni Au I Ka Wai*
- *Lovely Moloka'i*
- *On a Coconut Island*
- *The Carburetor Song*
- *Aloha Noooooo Waikiki*
- *Ainahau*
- *Aloha No au I Ko Maka*
- *Sweet Hawaiian Valentine*
- *My Little Grass Shack*
- *Red Opu*
- *Aloha 'Oe*

There were two sides to performer Charles K.L. Davis. A classically trained operatic tenor, he could belt out soaring arias and classic Hawaiian songs. Davis was equally known for his *kolohe* (rascal) local tunes, which he sang with just as much gusto as he performed the standards.

"He could do it all," said longtime Hawai'i radio deejay Harry B. Soria, Jr. "He could bang away at a piano at Kemo'o Farms and sing colorful songs with double entendre and, the next thing you know, he sings the classic 'Waialua.'"

Aloha – Charles K.L. Davis Sings and Plays for Hawai'i, an anthology of songs recorded in the '60s and '70s, demonstrated his versatility. The album contains everything from *hapa-haole* tunes such as "The Carburetor Song" to Queen Liliu'okalani's "Aloha 'Oe."

Davis drew musical inspiration from the classic show tunes he saw in movie theaters, as well as the Hawaiian music sung by *kupuna* (elders) at family *lū'au* held at his Waialua home. At age 25, Davis moved to New York to study at the prestigious Juilliard School. There, he focused on concert and operatic training, honing his golden tenor voice.

Davis' credits are as wide ranging as his vocal talent. He performed as a duo with singer-actor Jimmy Shigeta at Hollywood's Mocambo Café, co-starred in *My Fair Lady* with Broadway actress Patrice Munsel, and went on a month-long tour Russia with opera singer Risa Stevens for *The Ed Sullivan Show*.

One of Davis' biggest honors came in 1958, when he became one of the first Hawaiians to win the prestigious Metropolitan Opera auditions.

When he appeared on *The Dinah Shore Chevy Show* in the late '50s, the announcer introduced him as "the greatest voice in the Islands." It was a claim few would dispute – except to say that he was no slouch out of the Islands, either.

Davis left the glitz of Hollywood and New York City in the late 1960s. He headlined at the Monarch Room and, later, performed for 13 years at Kemo'o Farms, a piano lounge near Schofield Barracks.

"He was a comedian, but he could do so many wonderful things – Noel Coward songs, monarchy songs," longtime friend Nina Kealiiwahamana praised him. "He could make the old Hawaiians cry, because he would bring back memories with his wonderful, robust voice. He had so many accomplishments, but he could still come home and do a piano bar with such flair and such fun. He was just magnificent."

With his distinctive, robust voice, Charles K.L. Davis "could make the old Hawaiians cry."

50

THE BEST OF THE KAHAUANU LAKE TRIO, VOL. 1

The Kahauanu Lake Trio, 1983

The Best of the Kahauanu Lake Trio
KE PO'OKELA VOL. I

- *Pili Palua*
- *Wahine Hololio*
- *Pua Lililehua*
- *Pua Ahihi*
- *Lei Lokelani*
- *Hapa–Haole Hula Medley*
- *He Aloha No 'O Honolulu*
- *Mi Nei*
- *A 'Oia*
- *Kūliaikanu'u*
- *Maile Lau Li'i Li'i*
- *Ke Kali Nei Au*

From the 1950s to the '80s, the Kahauanu Lake Trio stirred audiences with their jazz-infused, acoustic performances of Hawaiian music. With Kahauanu's imaginative use of 'ukulele chords, his brother Tommy on acoustic bass and Al Machida on guitar – and with the Lake brothers able to sing both falsetto and naturally – the trio rarely sounded less than perfect.

The Best of the Kahauanu Lake Trio, Vol. 1, includes the group's biggest hit, "Pua Lililehua." Kahauanu wrote this ballad for his wife, the esteemed *kumu hula* Maiki Aiu Lake.

The anthology also showcases the group's knack for singing *hapa-haole* tunes, which they played with just as much as class and flair as they performed traditional Hawaiian songs. "Hapa-Haole Hula Medley" combines verses from three high-spirited compositions, "Hapa-Haole Hula Girl," "I Wonder Where My Little Hula Girl Has Gone" and "Hula Lolo."

"They were the prototype for what we now know as the modern Hawaiian trio – no steel, just 'ukulele, guitar and bass playing in a modern contemporary style of the day," said local radio personality Harry B. Soria, Jr. "They influenced every trio that recorded through the '70s, and they had a very deep, lasting impact."

Kahauanu's personal history sheds light on the complexity of the trio's music. His lineage is extensive, tracing back to Kamehameha I. His mother, a seventh-generation descendant of the warrior king, was adopted by Madame Alapa'i, the first singer of the Royal Hawaiian Band in 1873 under King Kalākaua.

"I think we started singing as soon as we came out of our mother," joked Kahauanu. "We were brought up with every top composer and musician in town coming to our house – Lena Machado, Bill Lincoln. Of course, we didn't realize who they were, but we got to hear these people. You get acquainted with their talent; before you know it, you must grab it and formulate your own."

While attending St. Mary's College in California, Kahauanu was introduced to another music genre: jazz. One of his favorite performers was Nat "King" Cole. Upon returning home after college, Kahauanu incorporated these jazz influences into his arrangements of traditional Hawaiian songs. It was a dynamic combination, buoyed by the top-notch skills of the trio's members, producing albums that have sold as well in the 21st century as they did decades earlier.

This open-air, oceanfront setting at the Halekūlani was the trio's long-time Waikīkī showcase. Left to right: Kahauanu Lake, Al Machida and Tommy Lake.

CREDITS

Mahalo to the artists and producers who provided record albums and album photography, and to the many people who contributed photographs and other memorabilia, with permission, as follows.

ii (top) Mountain Apple Co., (bottom left) Jeffrey Apaka, (bottom center) Hula Records, (bottom right) Olivier Koning photo/FilmWorks Pacific 5 (upper right) Karin Kovalsky photo 9-11 Tom Moffatt 13-15 Hula Records 17 Susan Titelman photo courtesy of Steve Siegfried and Panini Records, Inc. 18-19 Panini Records, Inc. 21 Ka'uhane Lee 22 Patricia Letuli 23 David Darling photo 25-27 Jim Linkner 29 Martin and Christina Denny 31 Tom Moffatt 32 Sharon Kaapana 33 Tom Moffatt 35 Mountain Apple Co. 36 Jimmy Forrest photo 37-41 Mountain Apple Co. 43 Malani Bilyeu 45 Hula Records 47 Jim Linkner 49-51 Buddy Fo 53-55 Mountain Apple Co. 57-59 Panini Records, Inc. 61-63 Jeffrey Apaka 65-67 Don Ho 69 Nina Kealiiwahamana 73 Mahi Beamer 74 Nathalie Walker photo 75 Mahi Beamer 77-79 Marlene Sai 81-83 Betty Kauhi 85 Mountain Apple Co. 87 Hula Records 89 Michael Cord International 91 Brett Uprichard photo 93 Ed Greevy photo 95-97 Hula Records 99 Tom Moffatt 101 Carol Miller-Keale 103 Mountain Apple Co. 105 Mountain Apple Co. 107-109 Robi Kahakalau 111 Hula Records 113-115 Melveen Leed 117 Mountain Apple Co. 119 Panini Records, Inc. 121-123 Emma Veary 125 Roy Sakuma 127 Melveen Leed 129 Lee Uyehara 131 Palani Vaughan 133 Ho'okena 135 Mountain Apple Co. 137 Jon Yamasato 139 Panini Records, Inc. 141 Mountain Apple 143 Martin and Christina Denny 145 Hula Records 147 Hula Records

Brothers Cazimero

Guava Jam

featuring Peter Moon

HAN...

...OUNG HAWAII PLAYS O...

...li'i Reichel

Honolulu City Lights

KEOLA & KAPONO BEAMER

Gabby

STEREO

FACING

Lomana

The Extraordinary
Kui Lee

Get On Home
The Days of My Youth
Ain't No Big Thing
If I Had It to Do All Over Again
Goin' Home
Kamakani Ka'ili Aloha
Rain, Rain Go Away
All I Want to Do
Yes, It's You 'Na Ali'i
I'll Remember You
No Other Song